Developmental Reading Assessment®

K–3

Second Edition

Joetta M. Beaver

In Collaboration With Primary Classroom Teachers

PEARSON

Author's Acknowledgments

The revision of the *Developmental Reading Assessment® K–3* is the result of much feedback, support, and encouragement from teachers, administrators, and other colleagues locally as well as across the United States and parts of Canada. Many thanks to the following:

The Upper Arlington City Schools' primary classroom and reading teachers for their initial work in the creation of the *DRA* from 1988 to 1996.

The 2005 Advisory Committee, consisting of Kathy McCulloch, Carol Price, Becky Ruf, Patti Schlaegel, and Kathleen Taps for their expertise, insights, suggestions, and encouragement.

All the teachers who field-tested the *DRA2, K–3,* materials and gave us feedback and suggestions for improving the assessment.

Beth Sycamore for her assistance with the revision of the teacher forms.

Dr. Jane Williams and Dr. Clement Stone for their leadership in the *DRA* pilots and field-tests over the years.

Kathleen Taps, Kathy McCulloch, Michelle Bell, Carol Price, Sue Wilder for their help with the Training DVD.

A special thank you to Kathleen Taps for her help selecting examples of students' written responses for the Handbook.

The following people have contributed to the development of this product:
Art and Design: Dorothea Fox, M. Jane Heelan, Dan Trush, Jennifer Visco, Heather Wendt Kemp
Editorial: Jaime Dritt, Donna Garzinsky, Teri Crawford Jones
Inventory: Yvette Higgins
Marketing: Andreea Cimoca, Ken Clinton
Production/Manufacturing: Jeff Engel, Pam Gallo, Suellen Leavy, Ruth Leine, John Rosta
Publishing Operations: Carolyn Coyle, Jennifer Van Der Heide
Technology: Jeff Wickersty

ISBN 13: 978-1-4284-0533-2
ISBN 10: 1-4284-0533-X

Printed in the United States of America

13 V059 11

Contents

Introduction

The number-one goal of any reading program should be to help students become proficient, enthusiastic readers who read for a variety of purposes. *Developmental Reading Assessment® K–8*, Second Edition, helps teachers achieve this goal for students in primary grades through middle school. *DRA2, K–3*, provides a method for assessing and documenting primary students' development as readers over time.

DRA2, K–3, enables primary teachers to systematically observe, record, and evaluate changes in student reading performance. *DRA2* provides teachers with information that helps them determine each student's independent reading level and identify what the student needs to learn next. The assessment can be used on a semi-annual or annual basis to monitor and document change over time in each student's reading. It may be used more frequently with struggling readers to ensure continued progress.

DRA2, K–3, is specially designed for kindergarten through third-grade classrooms with rich literate environments. In such classrooms, reading and writing are taught as reciprocal processes, a wide variety of children's books are available and accessible, and reading and writing activities are meaningful. On a daily basis, all students

- **hear a variety of literature read aloud**
- **read independently for a sustained period of time**
- **respond to literature in a variety of ways**
- **receive instruction and support in guided reading groups and/or individual reading conferences**

Joetta M. Beaver

Assessments are conducted during one-on-one reading conferences as children read specially selected assessment texts. *Developmental Reading Assessment, K–3*, provides Benchmark Assessment Books and Blackline Masters designed to guide the assessment. Within this Teacher Guide, you will find detailed assessment procedures, examples of different student responses, and general guidelines for instruction to address learning needs identified by *DRA2*.

If you are a current *DRA* user, you will also find highlighted in this Teacher Guide the many new features of the second edition. In addition to the *DRA2* assessment materials, the Second Edition includes a clipboard with a built-in timer and calculator for teachers to time students' oral readings and calculate scores. Improved Online Management System capabilities include an optional *DRA2*, Online Writer, the digital pen solution powered by Anoto® technology, and corresponding Teacher Observation Guides for fostering more efficient scoring.

Research Support for DRA and DRA2, K–3

The *Developmental Reading Assessment* for the first edition of K–3 was originally developed, field-tested, and revised in collaboration with classroom teachers and Joetta Beaver in the Upper Arlington City School District of Ohio between 1988 and 1996. The procedures, forms, and Benchmark Assessment Books have changed over the years (1998–2003) in response to multiple field-tests and feedback from teachers across the United States and parts of Canada. The goal of all revisions has been to create an effective, reliable, informative, and practical reading assessment for primary students.

In 1999, twenty new assessment texts and their coordinating forms were created. These were field-tested in May 2000 by teachers in school districts in the United States and Canada. Further revisions were made based on the participating teachers' feedback and suggestions. In September 2000, the newly revised texts and forms were field-tested, and a few additional revisions were made prior to publication.

In 1999–2000, a Spanish-language version of the original *DRA K–3*, *Evaluación del Desarrollo de la Lectura*, or *EDL*, was also created and field-tested.

The *DRA Word Analysis*, an individual diagnostic assessment, was added to the *DRA K–3* in 2004. *DRA Word Analysis* provides classroom and reading teachers with a systematic means to observe how struggling and emerging readers attend to and work with the various components of spoken and written words. This assessment was field-tested in the winter of 2003 and then again in the fall of 2003 by classroom and reading teachers across the United States. Their feedback and suggestions were used to further revise and modify the teacher directions and student forms.

DRA2 Pre-Publication Research

DRA K–3 was revised in collaboration with an advisory committee in central Ohio in 2005. The preliminary basis for revisions came from feedback and suggestions from other primary teachers and administrators who use *DRA*, and consultants who train teachers how to use *DRA*. The Second Edition includes

- revised assessment texts
- new fiction and nonfiction assessment texts
- an assessment process that is more uniform across *DRA K–8* levels but still developmentally appropriate for primary students

DRA2, K–3, was field-tested by primary classroom and reading teachers across the United States in the fall of 2004 and in the spring of 2005. The field test confirmed the following:

- The new Benchmark Assessment Books are in order of difficulty, and the texts at each level are comparable.
- The procedures and forms are easy for teachers to use in conducting the assessment and give teachers pertinent and relevant information to make instructional decisions.
- The Accuracy and Oral Reading Rate (starting at Level 14) scores are grouped appropriately for Emerging/Intervention, Developing/Instructional, Independent, and Advanced on the Continuum.
- The questions and prompts in the Student Booklets are developmentally appropriate at each level.

Technical Information on DRA2, K–3

DRA K–3 assesses student performance in the following areas of reading proficiency: reading engagement, oral reading fluency, and comprehension. The selection of these target skill areas and the methods used to assess them are based on current research in reading from sources such as the *National Reading Panel Report* (2000) and *Reading for Understanding* (Rand Education, 2002).

The Technical Manual for the first edition of *DRA K–3* contains information to support validity, reliability, predictive usefulness, and correlation to other known valid measures of reading achievement. Examples of the research included in the Technical Manual are as follows:

- **evidence that the number of students reading below grade level dropped dramatically after the implementation of *DRA* as a classroom evaluation tool**
- **a reliability analysis that demonstrates inter-rater reliability**
- **several validity studies supporting both the *DRA* and the *EDL* (Spanish version)**

This information will be revised and updated in 2006 to reflect current and ongoing research for the Second Edition.

To request the *Developmental Reading Assessment*® Technical Manual, please log on to www.pearsonschool.com or call 1-800-321-3106.

Good Readers and DRA2, K–3

To scaffold the process of learning to read, it is important to recognize the characteristics and behaviors of good readers and foster them in all of your students. Primary students are in the process of learning to read and respond to increasingly more complex texts. The *DRA2, K–3*, is based on what good readers do and scaffolds primary students as they move through the various stages of learning to read. *DRA2* supports the ongoing instruction of these students by providing you with pertinent information you can use to help all of your students become more proficient readers.

Good Readers . . .	In the *DRA2, K–3* . . .	Rationale
enjoy reading; have favorite books, authors, and genres; and generally have preferences about where and when they read. They talk about books and recommend their favorites.	**students respond to questions about what they are reading and their reading preferences.**	The Reading Engagement questions in *DRA2* (1) help teachers to become aware of students' preferences and (2) alert teachers to students who are somewhat passive about reading or have limited literacy experiences. It is important that students not only learn how to read but also find reading enjoyable.
select appropriately leveled reading materials for multiple purposes.	**students select a text that seems just right for them—not too easy and not too hard—from a range of three or four texts chosen by the teacher.**	Learning how to select appropriately leveled reading materials to fulfill multiple purposes enables students to (1) become more independent in the classroom and (2) have greater control over their choice of reading materials. When students are given opportunities to choose their own texts, they are more likely to read and enjoy reading.
read and sustain their independent reading for longer periods of time.	**teachers note the level of support needed by students during guided and independent reading.**	Students' ability to read increases as they spend time reading many texts at their independent reading level. Teaching students how to sustain independent reading for longer periods of time is an important part of a primary reading program.

Good Readers . . .	In the *DRA2, K–3* . . .	Rationale
use text features to help them preview a text.	**students use the title and illustrations in fiction texts or the title, table of contents, headings, and other graphic features in nonfiction texts to construct an initial idea of what they will be reading.**	Previewing a book actually makes reading easier. Reading the information on the cover and title page, leafing through the book to get a feel for the layout and text features, as well as briefly sampling parts of the text enable readers to predict and set expectations for their reading.
predict and pose questions before and while they read a text.	**after reading a designated passage, students predict what they think will happen in a fiction text or pose questions they think will be answered in a nonfiction text.**	Information gathered from the preview, along with prior knowledge, enables readers to predict (1) what might happen or (2) what they will learn. The readers' predictions and questions form a purpose for reading and a basis for monitoring comprehension.
read aloud in meaningful phrases with appropriate expression.	**teachers note students' phrasing, intonation, and attention to punctuation as they read orally.**	Reading fluently in longer, meaningful phrases with appropriate intonation supports (1) comprehension and (2) ease in reading longer, more complex texts.
read at an appropriate reading rate with a high percent of accuracy.	**as students read aloud, teachers (1) time students' oral reading to calculate their reading rates and (2) record students' miscues to determine a percent of accuracy.**	When students read texts that are "just right" fluently, they (1) find reading more enjoyable, (2) are able to focus more of their attention on constructing meaning, and (3) are more likely to develop a positive attitude toward reading.
use effective strategies and sources of information to problem-solve unknown words, monitor word choice, and self-correct significant miscues.	**teachers note observable reading behaviors (e.g., pausing, rereading, searching the illustrations, appealing for help, sounding out clusters of letters, self-correcting) as evidence of students' use of various strategies.**	When readers control and use a variety of strategies, they are able to quickly and effectively (1) decode words and (2) self-correct miscues. They are also more likely to (1) attend to meaning as well as (2) view themselves as good readers.

Good Readers . . .	In the *DRA2, K–3* . . .	Rationale
construct meaning as they read and then share/demonstrate their understanding either orally or in writing.	**students either (1) retell orally what they read or (2) write a summary in their own words.**	Constructing meaning before, during, and after reading a text is at the heart of reading. The ability to effectively (1) comprehend, and then (2) retell and/or (3) write a summary that includes important information (e.g., key concepts, facts, and vocabulary in a nonfiction text; key characters, events, and details in a fiction text) is essential for all successful readers/learners.
locate and use what is explicitly stated in a text.	**students locate and use information explicitly stated in the text to respond to a prompt.**	The ability to recall, locate, and use specific information stated in a text enables readers to (1) respond to literal questions, as well as (2) support opinions, and (3) justify responses.
make connections. They relate what they read to their own personal experiences, their understanding of the world, and other texts.	**students tell what a text makes them think of.**	Making connections with what they read enhances readers' (1) understanding of and at times (2) appreciation for a text. Connections to self, the world, and other texts support higher-level thinking, such as predicting, interpreting, comparing, contrasting, and evaluating. It also makes a text more memorable.
interpret what they read by making inferences.	**students tell or write about what they think was implied in a text in response to a question or prompt.**	The ability to go beyond the literal meaning of a text enables readers to gain a deeper understanding as they use prior knowledge to grasp the meaning of what is implied by the author.
determine importance and evaluate what they read.	**students identify what they think is the most important (1) message, (2) event, or (3) information in a text.**	Readers use their prior knowledge to help them (1) determine importance and (2) evaluate what they read. Students' abilities to establish and/or use criteria when making judgments are important skills in critical reading and thinking.
support their responses using information from a text and/or their own background knowledge.	**students give the reason(s) they identified an event, message, or idea as most important.**	The ability to justify one's response is an important skill for all readers and learners. It (1) enables others to know the basis for a decision and (2) provides an opening for further discussion.

Comparing the First Edition and the Second Edition of DRA K–3

The Second Edition adds new fiction and nonfiction Benchmark Assessment Books, replaces or revises some of the original Benchmark Assessment Books, and modifies the assessment procedures for transitional and extending readers so there is a smoother transition between the *DRA2, K–3,* and *DRA2, 4–8.* The following chart details the major differences between the First and Second Editions and gives an explanation for the improvement.

DRA K–3, First Edition	*DRA K–3,* Second Edition	Rationale for Change
The Benchmark Assessment Books range from Levels A to 44. (Note: Level 40 is a fourth-grade-level text and Level 44 is a fifth-grade-level text.)	**The Benchmark Assessment Books range from Level A to 40. The Second Edition includes four Level 40 texts from the *DRA2, 4–8,* set and no fifth-grade-level texts.**	In *DRA2,* students who are reading above grade level should read no more than one grade level above their present grade. For this reason, Level 44, a fifth-grade-level text, has been omitted from the Second Edition.
Teachers note students' oral reading fluency (phrasing and intonation) on the Teacher Observation Guides and *DRA Continuum.*	**Teachers time students' oral reading to determine their oral reading rate beginning with *DRA2* text Level 14.**	A slow reading rate not only hinders the reader's comprehension, but it also limits the amount read during the school day and throughout the year. Slow readers perceive themselves as poor readers, and they often do not enjoy reading.
Teachers stop the assessment if students' accuracy rate is below 94% on the Record of Oral Reading.	**Teachers stop the assessment if students' accuracy rate and/or oral reading rate fall below Developing/Independent on the *DRA2* Continuum.**	Research and *DRA2* field-test data indicate that appropriate oral reading rates and accuracy have an impact on students' ability to construct meaning.
Students give an oral retelling of what they have read and respond orally to all prompts and questions. The top score for Comprehension is 24.	**Students reading *DRA2* texts Level 28 and above write a one-page summary of what they've read as well as responses to Literal Comprehension, Interpretation, and Reflection questions or prompts within a Student Booklet. In the oral retelling and summary sections, vocabulary concepts are now part of the assessment, raising the top Comprehension score to 28.**	Most state assessments require students to respond to different types of questions and prompts in writing. *DRA2* provides insight into how well students respond in writing. The composing process gives students time to think about what is important to include and how to organize their thoughts. Knowledge of a student's control or understanding of words and concepts is important to the assessment of comprehension.
Teachers document students' progress on a Continuum folder.	**The Continuum is a part of the Teacher Observation Guide for each text.**	The inclusion of the Continuum within the Teacher Observation Guide allows for immediate marking of descriptors to determine students' strengths and needs.
Teachers find students' Independent DRA text level.	**Teachers find students' Independent *DRA2* text levels, however, clear guidelines are included on page 64 for teachers who are directed to find students' Instructional text levels.**	Some districts/state administrators have a need to identify students' Instructional text levels to meet other objectives.

Components of DRA2, K–3

This assessment package contains all of the materials shown below. These components are essential for conducting the assessment and analyzing student performance.

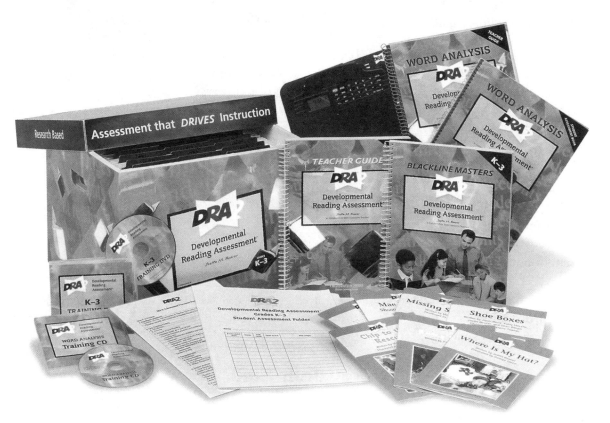

DRA2, _K–3_, Package includes:
Teacher Guide
Blackline Masters
Blackline Masters CD
45 Benchmark Assessment Books
30 Student Assessment Folders
Assessment Procedures Overview Card
DRA2 Clipboard
Training DVD
DRA Word Analysis Teacher Guide
DRA Word Analysis Student Book
DRA Word Analysis Training CD
DRA2 Organizer Box
46 Hanging File Folders

Also Available:
• *DRA2 Online Management System*
www.pearsonschool.com/dratour

• www.Connect2DRA.com

• *EDL2, K–6*

• *DRA2 Online Writer,* the digital pen solution powered by Anoto®, and
Teacher Observation Guide pages

Benchmark Assessment Books

Fiction Texts

The *DRA2, K–3,* Benchmark Assessment Books, Levels A–40, were carefully developed, field-tested, and revised to ensure that they are grade-level appropriate, in order of difficulty, and appealing to primary-grade students. They were created to reflect cultural diversity, include strong female and male characters, and represent a range of text difficulty. The following factors were also taken into consideration:

- concepts and experiences common to a majority of primary-grade children
- level of picture support
- inclusion of repetitive language, events, and/or episodes
- vocabulary and word choice
- sentence length and complexity
- print features such as length of text (number of words and lines of text per page), font size, and spacing

Level 1

Level 2

Levels A–2

- Benchmark Assessment Books for these levels consist of a repeated word or sentence pattern with natural language structures.

- The simple illustrations include animals and objects familiar to primary-grade children and highly support the text.

- One line of text appears on the left-hand page.

- The words are large and well spaced so that children are able to point as they read.

- The number of words in the texts ranges from 20 to 42.

Levels 3–6

- Benchmark Assessment Books for these levels consist of simple stories that contain repetitive words, phrases, and actions. They use mostly predictable language structures.

- The stories include characters and experiences that are familiar to primary-grade children, and pictures still provide much support.

- One to three lines of text are placed below each picture.

- The number of words in the texts ranges from 53 to 73.

Mom looked in the closet.
"It is not here," she said.

4

Ben looked in his toy box.
"It is not here," he said.
He looked and looked.

Level 4

One day Kevin's big brother got a new wagon. He used it to carry his newspapers.

Kevin liked the wagon, but he never got to ride in it.

2

Then one day Kevin's brother gave the wagon to their sister. She used the wagon for a sandbox.

Sometimes Kevin got to play in the wagon, but he never got to ride in it.

3

Level 14

Levels 8–14

- These Benchmark Assessment Books are stories about children and problems to which students can relate.

- There is some repetition of events in each of the stories.

- Book and oral-language structures are integrated, and the number of high-frequency words is expanded.

- The illustrations give moderate support, provide information about the setting, and suggest the sequence of events.

- The text, consisting of two to six lines, is located under the illustrations.

- The number of words in the texts ranges from 87 to 207.

Levels 16–28

- In these Benchmark Assessment Books, the characters are children with problems to which students can relate or animals with human characteristics.

- The content begins to move beyond students' personal experiences and builds a basis with which to compare and contrast other stories.

- Literary language structures are integrated with natural language.

- Some description of characters and settings are included.

- Illustrations provide moderate to minimum support.

- The text may be above or beneath the illustrations, or a full page.

- The number of words in these texts starts at 253 and increases with each level of difficulty up to 689 words.

Chip, the mouse, and Dot, the giraffe, were good friends. Dot took Chip out for rides.

"I'm on top of the world!" Chip called out.

Some giraffes didn't know why Dot was friends with such a tiny animal.

"Chip is so small," the tallest giraffe told Dot. "He can't do anything."

"Yes, he can," said Dot. "He is a good friend."

2

Sara put all of her stuffed animals in a packing box. Sneakers, her black cat with white paws, jumped off her bed. He reached up and put his front paws on the box.

"No, Sneakers, you're not going inside the box," Sara laughed. "We'll take you in your crate when we move."

Sara's mother peeked inside her room. "The moving truck is coming early tomorrow. Are you almost done packing?"

"Yes," said Sara. "I just need to pack up Sneakers' toys."

"Remember to put Sneakers in his crate first thing in the morning," her mother said. "We don't want to lose him during the move!"

Sara knew that watching her cat was an important job. Sneakers loved to sneak out of the house. He could be very hard to find!

2

DR 2

Chip to the Rescue

Written by Marcie Aboff
Illustrated by Jason Wolff

A Benchmark Assessment Book

Level 16

DR 2

Missing Sneakers

Written by Marcie Aboff
Illustrated by Bob Alley

A Benchmark Assessment Book

Level 28

Levels 30–38

- These Benchmark Assessment Books include realistic fiction, fantasy, and animal adventure.

- They are slightly more complex stories that include descriptions of settings, characters, problem(s), and resolution(s) in greater detail.

- Sentence length and vocabulary are more complex than in the previous text levels.

- Background knowledge and higher-level thinking skills are needed at times to understand and appreciate the humor, the problem, or the suspense in each story—as well as the character development.

- There is less picture support.

- Text size is slightly smaller and fills full pages or partial pages.

- The number of words ranges from 963 to 1,089.

Pedro started to wash Miss Clark's dishes while Ann gave Zane a bath.

"You both are working so hard," said Miss Clark.

"We're not working. We're helping," Pedro said.

"This is fun," added Ann.

"I promise to think of something special for you to do," said Miss Clark.

The next day Miss Clark handed Pedro a grocery list and some money. Then Miss Clark hooked Zane's leash to his collar and handed it to Ann.

"Zane could use a walk. Will you please take him with you?" she asked. "But don't ever leave him by himself," she added.

Pedro and Ann were very excited. They could barely keep from running to the store on the corner. Zane was excited, too. He was eager to see and smell everything. He barked at a butterfly and sniffed a tree. Ann held his leash tightly. Pedro held the grocery list and money tightly, too.

4

The mother beaver rested by the log dam for a moment. She watched her young son and daughter playing on the shore of the beaver pond. She was worried about them being on land. They belonged in the water. There they could move quickly. They could dive deep and swim underwater like two big, brown fish.

The mother beaver climbed out of the water. She began packing mud into the dam. Her hairless tail lay flat on the dam behind her, supporting her while she worked. Her strong front paws looked like little hands as they packed the mud into place.

Again and again, the mother beaver stopped working to watch her kits. Their father was far upstream, cutting down more trees for the dam.

She looked now and then toward the beavers' lodge, which was built of sticks and mud piled up in deep water. The round, mud-covered roof of the lodge rose above the water. Under the roof was a high, dry room that could be entered only from an underwater tunnel. This room was the safest place the beaver kits would ever know.

2

Busy Helpers

Written by Thea Feldman
Illustrated by Amy Wummer

A Benchmark Assessment Book

Level 30

Trouble at the Beaver Pond

Written by Frances and Dorothy Wood
Illustrated by Denny Bond

A Benchmark Assessment Book

Level 38

Level 40

Note: The Level 40 Benchmark Assessment Books are a part of *DRA*2, *4–8*, and are included in the *DRA*2, *K–3*, kit for third-grade students who are reading at a fourth-grade level.

• *All the Way Under*, a realistic fiction text, is about a young girl who is afraid to tell her cousin that she can't swim.

• *A Journey to Freedom*, a historical fiction text, is set in the mid-1800s and lightly touches on the subject of the Underground Railroad.

• These fourth-grade-level texts range in length from 1,325 to 1,359 words.

After a hard day of picking cotton, Jed went into the slave cabin. He lay down on the narrow board that was his bed. A few minutes later he heard his mother, Bess, come in. Jed expected to feel his mother's soft kiss and to hear her whisper, "Good night."

Instead, Jed heard her whisper, "We have to leave this place tonight. Master Boyd is dying. When I was sewing in the plantation house, I overheard Master Boyd's son. He said that he plans to sell some of the young slaves as soon as his father dies."

Jed shuddered. He knew that Master Boyd had promised never to separate him from his mother, but Mr. Boyd's son had made no such promise. Slave mothers and children were often separated, forever. His mother had always told him that she would never let that happen. But what could his mother do to prevent it?

"Get up, Jed," said his mother. "Get your coat and hat, and be as quiet as you can. Not a word until I tell you it's safe!"

Jed quickly grabbed his things and followed his mother. Jed was sure his beating heart would wake the others before they left the rundown slave cabin.

Bess held her son's hand tightly as they darted for the woods. Jed stumbled along after his mother. His mind was full of questions. Where were they running to? How did his mother know which way to run? Neither of them had ever been outside of the plantation. ✳

After what seemed like forever, Bess finally slowed down. Holding her finger to her lips, she pointed to a spot behind a clump of evergreen trees. The two of them dropped down on a bed of pine needles.

3

A Journey to Freedom

Written by Rose Howell
Illustrated by Joanne Friar

A Benchmark Assessment Book

Level 40

Nonfiction Texts

As students learn to read, it is important that they learn how to read nonfiction texts. For this reason, nonfiction Benchmark Assessment Books are included at Levels 16, 28, 38, and 40 in *DRA2, K–3*, so that you can assess how well students preview, read, and comprehend informational texts, and use graphic features to access and recall information.

In addition to the factors used to level fiction texts, the following factors were used to determine the level of difficulty for nonfiction texts:

- number of concepts/topics and supporting facts presented
- number of multi-syllable content-related vocabulary words

- number and types of headings
- number and variety of graphic features

All of the nonfiction Benchmark Assessment Books include colorful photographs as well as information presented graphically in the form of timelines, flowcharts, maps, comparison charts, and/or diagrams. Text Levels 28, 38, and 40 also include:

- table of contents
- glossary
- boldfaced glossary words in the main text

Level 16

- The nonfiction Benchmark Assessment Books at Level 16 (end of first grade) include *Animal Homes* and *Baby Birds*.

- These topics and the vocabulary are familiar to many primary-grade children.

- The texts mainly consist of simple sentences and some repetitive phrases.

- A chart on the final page(s) categorizes the information presented in the text.

- One to four lines of text appear under the photographs. The texts range in length from 174 to 177 words.

Birds keep their eggs warm.

Mother robin sits on the nest to keep the eggs warm. She turns the eggs every day.

Mother robin sits on the nest for about 13 days. Father robin stays nearby.

7

DRA2

Baby Birds

Written by Peggy DeLapp

A Benchmark Assessment Book

Level 16

Animal Helpers

Animals that are a part of the family are called pets. Some people have pets like dogs, cats, birds, or rabbits. Other people have animals that are more than just pets.

Animals Can Help
Written by Lisa Trumbauer

These ani...
help peop...
and get st...
see, hear,...

A Benchmark Assessment Book

Level 28

Level 28

- The Level 28 (end of second grade) nonfiction Benchmark Assessment Books are *From Peanuts to Peanut Butter* and *Animals Can Help*.

- The topics and much of the vocabulary are familiar to primary-grade children. The text includes some compound and complex sentences.

- Two to seven lines of text appear above or below the photographs or other graphics. The texts range in length from 423 to 425 words.

Level 38

- The Level 38 (end of third grade) nonfiction Benchmark Assessment Books, *Slammin' Sammy* and *Mae Jemison*, are biographies.

- The topics and specialized vocabulary may be familiar to primary-grade students.

- The texts consist of a variety of sentence lengths and structures.

- Four to twelve lines of text appear above or below the photographs, illustrations, or other graphics. The texts range in length from 819 to 831 words.

Mae's Space Training

In 1987, Mae was selected to be in the astronaut training program. Only fifteen people were picked. Mae was one of them.

Mae trained at the space center in Texas for one year. Mae had to learn how to live and work in space. She also needed to learn about the **space shuttle** and how it works.

Mae being suited up

Mae learning about the shuttle

Mae Jemison
Shooting for the Stars
Written by Sarah Tatler

A Benchmark Assessment Book

Mae and other astronauts floating inside a special training jet

Mae flew in a special training jet. The jet would climb very high and then go into a steep **dive**. When it started to dive, Mae felt like she was in space. She floated around the special padded cabin. She practiced tasks like eating and drinking while floating in the air.

To learn more about how to move in space, Mae trained in large water tanks wearing a special suit. The training was difficult, but it helped Mae learn what it feels like to be in space. It also taught her how to work with different parts of the shuttle.

6   7

Level 38

The Amazing Octopus
Written by Vicki León

A Benchmark Assessment Book

Level 40

The Octopus

Deep in the ocean lives a creature known for its tricks. It can get out of the tightest places. It can change its shape and its color in less than a second. This creature is **coldblooded** and is called an octopus. More than 150 kinds of octopuses can be found around the world. The smallest is the size of a thumb. The biggest is more than 20 feet from arm tip to arm tip.

An octopus has no **backbone**. It has a body shaped like a balloon that is covered by a **mantle**. It has eight arms. Each arm has rows of **suckers**. Most kinds of octopuses have about 2,000 suckers. These suckers help an octopus to pick up and eat food. They also help it to cling to a hiding place. Octopus arms are always busy. They use their arms to walk, crawl, dig, and eat.

An octopus has two eyes. It can turn its eyes in half circles without moving its head. Its eyesight is very sharp. An octopus uses **gills** and a **funnel** for breathing. Its funnel also helps the octopus move through water. ✦

Parts of an Octopus

arms
funnel
eyes
mantle
suckers

2   3

Level 40

- The fourth-grade nonfiction Benchmark Assessment Books are *The Amazing Octopus* and *A Pack of Wolves*. These books include interesting facts about each animal.

- The texts use a variety of sentence lengths and structures.

- These texts range in length from 941 to 992 words and have some full pages of text.

Assessment Forms

DRA2, K–3, includes a number of assessment forms for assessing students' reading and for recording their progress over time. The forms, which can be photocopied for classroom use, are included in the Blackline Masters book. They are also available as printable PDF documents on the *DRA2* Blackline Masters CD included in your kit and via the *DRA2 Online Management System*.

Teacher Observation Guides

Each Benchmark Assessment Book has its own Teacher Observation Guide. The guides include teacher directions, questions, and prompts for the assessment texts. Teachers will record observations of a student's reading behaviors as well as their responses in the designated spaces.

① This section is used to record scores for each section at the end of the assessment.

② Student responses are recorded next to the Reading Engagement questions. Starting at Level 28, students will complete a Student Reading Survey.

③ The bold, italicized print is what you read or say to the student.

④ In the Introduction and Preview, for Levels 4–16, students do a "picture walk."

⑤ The oral reading is timed, starting with Level 14.

⑥ The student's miscues, including substitutions, omissions, and insertions, as well as repetitions and self-corrections are marked on the Record of Oral Reading.

Teacher Observation Guide   **The Wagon**   Level 14, Page 1

Name/Date _____   Teacher/Grade _____

① **Scores:**   Reading Engagement ___/8   Oral Reading Fluency ___/16   Comprehension ___/28
Independent Range: 6–7   11–14   19–25

Book Selection   Text selected by: ☐ teacher   ☐ student

1. READING ENGAGEMENT

(If the student has recently answered these questions, skip this section.)

② *T: Tell me about one of your favorite books.* _____

T: Would you rather read ☐ *alone,* ☐ *with a buddy, or* ☐ *with a group?*

Why? _____

③ *T: Whom do you read with at home?* _____

2. ORAL READING FLUENCY

④ **INTRODUCTION AND PREVIEW**

T: In this story, The Wagon, *Kevin's two brothers and his sister use the same wagon for different things. Look at the pictures, and tell me what is happening in this story.*

Note the student's use of connecting words (e.g., *and, then, but*) and vocabulary relevant to the text. You may use general prompts, such as "Now what is happening?" or "Turn the page," but do <u>not</u> ask specific questions. Tally the number of times you prompt.

RECORD OF ORAL READING ⏱ ⑤

Record the student's oral reading behaviors. Note the student's fluency (expression and phrasing). Be sure to time the student's reading.

T: The Wagon. *Now, read to find out how Kevin's brothers and sister fix the dented, dirty wagon when it is his turn to have it.*

Page 2

One   day   Kevin's   big   brother   got   a

⑥ new   wagon.   He   used   it   to   carry

his   newspapers.

Kevin   liked   the   wagon,   but   he   never

got   to   ride   in   it.

88

The Wagon 14

(7) After the student finishes reading, the oral reading time is recorded.

(8) The words-per-minute range is based on the oral reading time.

(9) All miscues that are not self-corrected in the Record of Oral Reading are counted and the number is circled on the chart to determine the student's percentage of accuracy.

(10) The assessment is stopped if the student's score falls in the shaded areas (Intervention and Instructional levels) for either words-per-minute or accuracy. Reassess the student with a lower level text immediately or at another time.

Teacher Observation Guide   *The Wagon*   Level 14, Page 3

Page 7

They   washed   the   wagon   with   the   water.
They   took   out   the   dents   with   the   hammer.
They   painted   the   wagon   a   nice   bright   green.
The   wagon   looked   better   than   new   because
it   had   Kevin's   name   on   it.

(7) Time: _____ minutes:seconds

ORAL READING WORDS PER MINUTE, PERCENT OF ACCURACY
Use the student's oral reading time to circle the WPM range.

Word Count: 202

	INTRVN	INSTR	IND	ADV
Minutes:Seconds	6:51 or more	6:50–5:07	5:06–2:52	2:51 or less
WPM	29 or less	30–39	40–70	71 or more

Count the number of miscues that are not self-corrected. Circle the percent of accuracy based on the number of miscues.

	INTRVN	INSTR	IND				ADV	
Number of Miscues	14 or more	12–13	10–11	8–9	6–7	4–5	1–3	0
Percent of Accuracy	93 or less	94	95	96	97	98	99	100

- If the student's score falls in a shaded area for either WPM or Accuracy, STOP! Reassess with a lower-level text.
- If the student is reading below the grade-level benchmark, administer *DRA Word Analysis*, beginning with Task 16, at another time.

The Wagon

90

11 For Levels 4–24, students orally retell the story. For Levels 28–40, students write a story summary.

12 A Story Overview is provided to record what students include in their retellings.

13 Teachers place checkmarks beside each question or prompt to indicate how much support was given during the retelling. No other prompts are permitted.

14 Response questions and prompts provide students with an opportunity to express their thoughts or opinions and reveal what kind of connections they make.

Teacher Observation Guide **The Wagon** Level 14, Page 4

3. COMPREHENSION

11 RETELLING

As the student retells, underline and record on the Story Overview the information included in the student's retelling. Please note the student does not need to use the exact words.

T: Close the book before the retelling, and then say: ***Start at the beginning, and tell me what happened in this story.***

12 Story Overview

Beginning

1. Kevin's big brother gets a new wagon; he carries newspapers in it—but Kevin never gets to ride in it.

Middle

2. Brother gives the wagon to his sister; she uses it for a sandbox—but Kevin never gets to ride in it.

3. Sister gives the wagon to their other brother; he uses it for a fort—but Kevin never gets to ride in it.

4. Brother gives the wagon to Kevin. Kevin is happy.

5. The wagon is old and dirty and has dents in it.

6. Brothers and sister wash the wagon, take out the dents, and paint it bright green.

End

7. The wagon looks better than new because it has Kevin's name on it.

13 If the retelling is limited, use one or more of the following prompts to gain further information. Place a checkmark by a prompt each time it is used.

☐ *Tell me more.*
☐ *What happened at the beginning?*
☐ *What happened before/after* _____ (an event mentioned by the student)*?*
☐ *Who else was in the story?*
☐ *How did the story end?*

REFLECTION

14 Record the student's responses to the prompts and questions below.

T: *What part did you like best in this story? Tell me why you liked that part.*

MAKING CONNECTIONS

...ent makes a text-to-self connection in his or her response to the above prompt, ...g question.

...ry make you think of? or *What connections did you make while reading this story?*

Teacher Observation Guide **The Wagon** Level 14, Page 5

4. TEACHER ANALYSIS

ORAL READING

15 If the student had 5 or more different miscues, use the information recorded on the Record of Oral Reading to complete the chart below.

Student problem-solves words using:	Number of miscues self-corrected: _____ Number of miscues not self-corrected: _____ Number of words told to the student: _____	
☐ beginning letter(s)/sound(s) ☐ letter-sound clusters ☐ onset and rime ☐ blending letters/sounds ☐ knowledge of spelling patterns (analogies) ☐ syllables ☐ rereading ☐ no observable behaviors	**Miscues interfered with meaning:** ☐ never ☐ at times ☐ often	**Miscues included:** ☐ omissions ☐ insertions ☐ substitutions that were 　☐ visually similar 　☐ not visually similar
Copy each substitution to help analyze the student's attention to visual information. e.g., <u>older</u> (substitution) 　　　other (text)		

16 **Oral Reading Rate:** (Optional) Use the formula below to determine the student's exact oral reading rate. Convert the student's reading time to all seconds.

202 (words) ÷ _____ total seconds = _____ WPS × 60 = _____ WPM

17 *DRA2* **Continuum**

• Circle the descriptors that best describe the student's reading behaviors and responses.
　1. Use your daily classroom observations and the student's responses to the Reading Engagement questions to select statements that best describe the student's level of Reading Engagement.
　2. Use your recorded observations from this assessment to select the statements that best describe the student's Oral Reading Fluency and Comprehension.
• Add the circled numbers to obtain a total score for each section.
• Record the total scores at the top of page 1.
Note: If the Comprehension score is less than 19, administer *DRA2* with a lower-level text.

---

15 The reading behaviors that match the student's oral reading performance are recorded on the chart. Specific miscue information is also recorded.

16 The optional formula provides the student's exact reading rate.

17 Instructions on how to complete the Continuum are provided.

DRA2 Continuum

The Continuum is now part of each Teacher Observation Guide and has been customized for each Benchmark Assessment Book as in the DRA2, 4–8. The book-specific Continuum scaffolds teachers' analysis of students' level of performance in Reading Engagement, Oral Reading Fluency, and Printed Language Concepts/Comprehension. A series of statements or descriptions reflects a range of possible behaviors and responses across four performance levels:

- **Emerging (Levels A–12)**
  Intervention (Levels 14–40)
- **Developing (Levels A–12)**
  Instructional (Levels 14–40)
- **Independent (Levels A–40)**
- **Advanced (Levels 4–40)**

The descriptors on the Continuum not only indicate the student's level of performance but also suggest a level of support.

Using the information recorded on the Teacher Observation Guide, you will be circling the statements that best describe the student's reading behaviors and/or responses in Reading Engagement, Oral Reading Fluency, and Printed Language Concepts/Comprehension.

After circling the selected statements on the Continuum, the circled numbers of the descriptors are added to determine the student's overall performance in Reading Engagement, Oral Reading Fluency, and Printed Language Concepts/Comprehension.

The student's total score in Oral Reading Fluency and Printed Language Concepts/Comprehension will determine if the text read is an independent, instructional, or advanced level.

- Independent: Total score for Oral Reading Fluency <u>and</u> Printed Language Concepts/Comprehension must be at least within the Independent range on the Continuum.
- Instructional: Total score for Oral Reading Fluency <u>or</u> Printed Language Concepts/Comprehension is within the Instructional range on the Continuum.
- Advanced: Total score for Oral Reading Fluency <u>and</u> Printed Language Concepts/Comprehension must be within the Advanced range on the Continuum.

Circled descriptors that fall within the Instructional or Intervention columns indicate a need for instruction or intervention. Circled descriptors that fall within the Independent and Advanced columns indicate strengths and areas to reinforce and extend. Use the descriptors selected on the Continuum to identify the student's instructional needs.

Fiction Continuum

In the Emergent stage, the Continuum focuses on oral reading and printed language concepts. Comprehension is added to the Continuum in the Early stage, beginning with Level 4. In Levels 4–24, up through the Transitional stage, Comprehension is based on oral responses. Starting with Level 28, Comprehension is based on written responses.

(1) Descriptors within Emerging or Intervention (1) indicate that these students do not understand what to do or lack the strategies and skills needed to adequately respond. These students require highly effective ongoing instruction and support so that confusions can be eliminated and effective skills and strategies can be learned and practiced.

(2) Descriptors within Developing or Instructional (2) indicate that these students have some control of the necessary strategies and skills to decode, comprehend, and respond to the prompts and questions for the assessed text level. They need models and demonstrations of what is expected. They should also have opportunities to learn and practice effective strategies and skills in order to function independently.

(3) Descriptors within Independent (3) suggest that these students for the most part control the necessary strategies and skills to decode, comprehend, and respond adequately to the prompts and questions for the assessed text level. They generally need instruction and scaffolding to extend their thinking and enhance their responses.

(4) Advanced (4) descriptors represent students who read fluently and demonstrate a deeper level of comprehension with thoughtful responses. They also demonstrate a high level of reading engagement. These students benefit from opportunities to read a variety of texts and to interact in groups to develop their critical literacy skills.

Name/Date _____ Teacher/Grade _____ Level 14, Page 6

DRA2 CONTINUUM **1**	LEVEL 14 **2**	**3** TRANSITIONAL READER	
INTERVENTION	**INSTRUCTIONAL**	**INDEPENDENT**	**ADVANCED** **4**
Reading Engagement			
Book Selection	1 Selects texts from identified leveled sets with teacher support; uncertain about a favorite book	2 Selects texts from identified leveled sets with moderate support; tells about favorite book in general terms	3 Selects texts from identified leveled sets most of the time; identifies favorite book by title and tells about a particular event	4 Selects a variety of "just right" texts; identifies favorite book by title and gives an overview of the book
Sustained Reading	1 Sustains independent reading for a short period of time with much encouragement	2 Sustains independent reading with moderate encouragement	3 Sustains independent reading for at least 10–15 minutes at a time	4 Sustains independent reading for an extended period of time
Score	2 3	4 5	6 7	8
Oral Reading Fluency			
Expression	1 No expression; monotone	2 Little expression; rather monotone	3 Some expression	4 Expression conveys meaning most of the time
Phrasing	1 Mostly word-by-word	2 Short phrases most of the time; inappropriate pauses	3 Longer word phrases some of the time; heeds most punctuation	4 Longer, meaningful phrases most of the time; heeds all punctuation
Rate	1 29 WPM or less	2 30–39 WPM	3 40–70 WPM	4 71 WPM or more
Accuracy	1 93% or less	2 94%	3 95%–98%	4 99%–100%
Score	4 5 6	7 8 9 10	11 12 13 14	15 16
Comprehension			
Previewing	1 Comments briefly about each event or action only when prompted or is uncertain	2 Identifies and comments briefly about each event or action with some prompting	3 Identifies and connects at least 3 key events without prompting; some relevant vocabulary	4 Identifies and connects at least 4 key events without prompting; relevant vocabulary
Retelling: Sequence of Events	1 Includes only 1 or 2 events or details (limited retelling)	2 Includes at least 3 events, generally in random order (partial retelling)	3 Includes most of the important events from the beginnning, middle, and end, generally in sequence	4 Includes all important events from the beginning, middle, and end in sequence
Retelling: Characters and Details	1 Refers to characters using general pronouns; may include incorrect information	2 Refers to characters using appropriate pronouns; includes at least 1 detail; may include some misinterpretation	3 Refers to most characters by name and includes some important details	4 Refers to all characters by name and includes all important details
Retelling: Vocabulary	1 Uses general terms or labels; limited understanding of key words/concepts	2 Uses some language/ vocabulary from the text; some understanding of key words/concepts	3 Uses language/ vocabulary from the text; basic understanding of most key words/concepts	4 Uses important language/vocabulary from the text; good understanding of key words/concepts
Retelling: Teacher Support	1 Retells with 5 or more questions or prompts	2 Retells with 3 or 4 questions or prompts	3 Retells with 1 or 2 questions or prompts	4 Retells with no questions or prompts
Reflection	1 Gives an unrelated response, no reason for opinion, or no response	2 Gives a limited response and/or a general reason for opinion	3 Gives a specific story event/action and a relevant reason for response (e.g., personal connection)	4 Gives a response and reason that reflects higher-level thinking (e.g., synthesis/inference)
Making Connections	1 Makes an unrelated connection, relates an event in the story, or gives no response	2 Makes a connection that reflects a limited understanding of the story	3 Makes a literal connection that reflects a basic understanding of the story	4 Makes a thoughtful connection that reflects a deeper understanding of the story
Score	7 8 9 10 11 12 13	14 15 16 17 18	19 20 21 22 23 24 25	26 27 28

Choose three to five teaching/learning activities on the *DRA2* Focus for Instruction on the next page.

The Wagon **14**

93

Nonfiction Continuum

For Levels 16, 28, 38, and 40, there are two kinds of Continuums, one for fiction texts and one for nonfiction texts. Some of the descriptors are similar on both Continuums. The descriptors that are not similar differ in that they reflect what students are expected to do and gain from informational or narrative texts.

Nonfiction Continuum

Level 38, Page 5

Name/Date _____ Teacher/Grade _____

Comprehension Score
38: _____

DRA2 CONTINUUM	LEVEL 38		EXTENDING READER	
	INTERVENTION	INSTRUCTIONAL	INDEPENDENT	ADVANCED
Reading Engagement				
Wide Reading	1 Title(s) below grade level; limited reading experiences and book knowledge	2 Titles slightly below grade level; rather limited reading experiences	3 Titles within 2 genres or multiple books within a genre; generally on-grade-level texts	4 Titles across 3 or more genres; many on- and above-grade-level texts
Self-Assessment/ Goal Setting	1 No strengths and/or goals	2 General strength(s) and goal(s) related to the reading process	3 2 specific strengths and 2 specific goals related to the reading process	4 3 specific strengths and 3 specific goals that reflect a higher level of thinking
Score	2 3	4 5	6 7	8
Oral Reading Fluency				
Expression	1 Little expression; monotone	2 Some expression that conveys meaning	3 Expression emphasizing key phrases and words at times	4 Expression emphasizing key phrases and words most of the time
Phrasing	1 Mostly word-by-word	2 Short phrases most of the time; inappropriate pauses	3 Longer phrases most of the time; heeds most punctuation	4 Consistently longer, meaningful phrases; heeds all punctuation
Rate	1 69 WPM or less	2 70–89 WPM	3 90–125 WPM	4 126 WPM or more
Accuracy	1 94% or less	2 95%	3 96%–98%	4 99%–100%
Score	4 5 6	7 8 9 10	11 12 13 14	15 16
Comprehension				
Prediction	1 Unrelated question(s) or no response	2 At least 1 reasonable question related to the text	3 At least 2 reasonable questions that go beyond page(s) read aloud	4 3 thoughtful questions that go beyond page(s) read aloud
Nonfiction Text Features	1 Limited information accessed from text features or no response	2 Partial information accessed from text features	3 Accurate information accessed from text features	4 Detailed information accessed from text features
Scaffolded Summary	1 1–2 ideas/facts in own language and/or copied text; may include incorrect information	2 Partial summary; generally in own language; some important ideas/facts; may include misinterpretations	3 Summary in own language; includes important ideas and a few supporting facts from each section	4 Summary in own language; includes the most important ideas and some supporting facts from each section
Scaffolded Summary: Vocabulary	1 General terms or labels; limited understanding of key words/concepts	2 Some language/ vocabulary from the text; some understanding of key words/concepts	3 Most language/ vocabulary from the text; basic understanding of most key words/concepts	4 All important language/vocabulary from the text; good understanding of key words/concepts
Literal Comprehension	1 Incorrect response or no response	2 Partial response; may include misinterpretation	3 Accurate response	4 Accurate response with specific details
Interpretation	1 Little or no understanding of important text implications	2 Some understanding of important text implications; no supporting details	3 Understands important text implications; may include supporting details	4 Insightful understanding of important text implications with supporting details or rationale
Reflection	1 Insignificant message; no reason for opinion or no response	2 Less significant message and/or a general reason for opinion	3 Significant message and a relevant reason for opinion	4 Significant message and reason for opinion that reflects higher-level thinking
Score	7 8 9 10 11 12 13	14 15 16 17 18	19 20 21 22 23 24 25	26 27 28

Choose three to five teaching/learning activities on the *DRA2* Focus for Instruction on the next page.

Slammin' Sammy 38

245

Fiction Continuum

Name/Date _____ Teacher/Grade _____

DRA2 CONTINUUM	LEVEL 38		
	INTERVENTION	INSTRUCTIONAL	INDEPEND...
Reading Engagement			
Wide Reading	1 Title(s) below grade level; limited reading experiences and book knowledge	2 Titles slightly below grade level; rather limited reading experiences	3 Titles within 2 multiple books w... genre; generally o... level texts
Self-Assessment/ Goal Setting	1 No strengths and/or goals	2 General strength(s) and goal(s) related to the reading process	3 2 specific stre... specific goals rel... reading process
Score	2 3	4 5	6 7
Oral Reading Fluency			
Expression	1 Little expression; monotone	2 Some expression that conveys meaning	3 Expression reflects mood, pace, and tension at times	4 Expression reflects mood, pace, and tension most of the time
Phrasing	1 Mostly word-by-word	2 Short phrases most of the time; inappropriate pauses	3 Longer phrases most of the time; heeds most punctuation	4 Consistently longer, meaningful phrases; heeds all punctuation
Rate	1 69 WPM or less	2 70–89 WPM	3 90–125 WPM	4 126 WPM or more
Accuracy	1 94% or less	2 95%	3 96%–98%	4 99%–100%
Score	4 5 6	7 8 9 10	11 12 13 14	15 16
Comprehension			
Use of Text Features	1 Limited or no description of the characters	2 Partial description of the characters; general statements	3 Description of each character; includes at least 2 specific details	4 Description of each character; includes at least 3 specific details
Prediction	1 Unrelated predictions or no response	2 At least 1 reasonable prediction related to the text	3 At least 2 reasonable predictions that go beyond the text read aloud	4 3 thoughtful predictions that go beyond the text read aloud
Scaffolded Summary	1 1–2 events in own language and/or copied text; may include incorrect information	2 Partial summary; generally in own language; some important characters/events; may include misinterpretations	3 Summary in own language; includes important characters, many of the important events, and some details from the beginning, middle, and end	4 Summary in own language; includes all important characters, events, and details from the beginning, middle, and end
Scaffolded Summary: Vocabulary	1 General terms or labels; limited understanding of key words/concepts	2 Some language/ vocabulary from the text; some understanding of key words/concepts	3 Most language/ vocabulary from the text; basic understanding of most key words/concepts	4 All important language/vocabulary from the text; good understanding of key words/concepts
Literal Comprehension	1 Incorrect response or no response	2 Partial response; may include misinterpretation	3 Accurate response	4 Accurate response with specific details
Interpretation	1 Little or no understanding of important text implications	2 Some understanding of important text implications; no supporting details	3 Understands important text implications; may include supporting details	4 Insightful understanding of important text implications with supporting details or rationale
Reflection	1 Insignificant event; no reason for opinion or no response	2 Less significant event and/or a general reason for opinion	3 Significant event and a relevant reason for opinion	4 Significant event and reason for opinion that reflects higher-level thinking
Score	7 8 9 10 11 12 13	14 15 16 17 18	19 20 21 22 23 24 25	26 27 28

Choose three to five teaching/learning activities on the *DRA2* Focus for Instruction on the next page.

A Trip Through Time 38

254

DRA2 Focus for Instruction

After completing the Continuum in the Teacher Observation Guide, the Focus for Instruction on the last page of the guide is used to determine what students need to learn next. This tool provides a checklist of activities/learning experiences based on the same categories used in the Continuum.

1 Three to five activities on the Focus for Instruction that address specific areas on the Continuum where the student's responses fell below the Independent range are selected.

Fiction

DRA2 FOCUS FOR INSTRUCTION FOR TRANSITIONAL READERS

READING ENGAGEMENT

Book Selection
- ☐ Teach student strategies to select "just right" texts for independent reading
- ☐ Introduce student to reading materials from a variety of genres
- ☐ Model and discuss why readers have favorite books and authors

Sustained Reading
- ☐ Model and support the use of sustained reading time
- ☐ Develop clear expectations for amount of independent reading
- ☐ Provide opportunities for buddy reading
- ☐ Create structures and routines to support reading at home

ORAL READING FLUENCY

Expression and Phrasing
- ☐ Have student practice appropriate phrasing and expression with familiar texts
- ☐ Model and support reading in longer meaningful phrases with appropriate expression
- ☐ Model and teach how to heed punctuation
- ☐ Have student participate in choral reading and/or reader's theater

Rate
- ☐ Provide materials and time for repeated reading to increase reading rate
- ☐ Teach student to read lower level and/or familiar texts at an appropriate rate

Accuracy: Word Analysis
- ☐ Support and reinforce self-corrections of miscues
- ☐ Model and support how to take words apart (onset and rime, syllables) to problem-solve unknown words
- ☐ Teach how to use word chunks and analogies to problem-solve unknown words
- ☐ Provide spelling activities and word sorts to help student recognize patterns in words

COMPREHENSION

Previewing
- ☐ Support creating a story from the illustrations
- ☐ Model and support previewing a book during read-aloud and shared reading experiences

Retelling
- ☐ Model and teach how to retell a story
- ☐ Model and teach how to identify important events to include in a retelling
- ☐ Support retelling a story in sequence
- ☐ Encourage student to use characters' names when retelling a story
- ☐ Model and teach how to identify important details to include in a retelling
- ☐ Model and support using key vocabulary/language from the text in a retelling
- ☐ Model and teach how to create and use story maps to aid retelling

Reflection
- ☐ Support and reinforce student's responses to books
- ☐ Provide opportunities to select a favorite book, toy, TV show, etc., and tell why it is a favorite
- ☐ Help student identify favorite part of books
- ☐ Demonstrate how to support one's opinion

Making Connections
- ☐ Model and teach how to make text-to-self connections
- ☐ Model and teach how to make text-to-text connections

OTHER

_____
_____
_____
_____
_____
_____
_____

The Wagon 14

Nonfiction

Baby Birds 16

DRA2 FOCUS FOR INSTRUCTION FOR TRANSITIONAL READERS

READING ENGAGEMENT

Book Selection
- ☐ Teach student strategies to select "just right" texts for independent reading
- ☐ Introduce student to reading materials from a variety of genres
- ☐ Model and discuss why readers have favorite books and authors

Sustained Reading
- ☐ Model and support the use of sustained reading time
- ☐ Develop clear expectations for amount of independent reading
- ☐ Provide opportunities for buddy reading
- ☐ Create structures and routines to support reading at home

ORAL READING FLUENCY

Expression and Phrasing
- ☐ Model and teach how to emphasize key words and phrases when reading informational texts
- ☐ Model and support reading in longer, meaningful phrases with appropriate expression
- ☐ Model and support how to attend to punctuation
- ☐ Have student practice appropriate phrasing and expression with familiar texts

Rate
- ☐ Provide materials and time for repeated reading to increase reading rate
- ☐ Teach student to read lower level and/or familiar texts at an appropriate rate

Accuracy Rate: Word Analysis
- ☐ Support and reinforce self-corrections of miscues
- ☐ Model and support how to take words apart (e.g., onset and rime, syllables) to problem-solve unknown words
- ☐ Teach how to use word chunks and analogies to problem-solve unknown words
- ☐ Provide spelling activities and word sorts to help student recognize patterns in words

COMPREHENSION

Previewing
- ☐ Model and support previewing informational books during read-aloud and shared reading experiences
- ☐ Model and teach student how to activate relevant background knowledge before reading an informational text

Retelling
- ☐ Model and teach how to retell the ideas and facts presented in an informational text
- ☐ Model and teach how to identify important information (key ideas and facts) to include in a retelling
- ☐ Support retelling information in a logical order
- ☐ Model and support using key vocabulary/language from the text in a retelling
- ☐ Model and support going back into the text for specific information

Using Nonfiction Text Features
- ☐ Teach student how to read information presented graphically
- ☐ Teach student how to use graphic organizers to keep track and present facts and ideas

Making Connections
- ☐ Model and teach how to make text-to-self connections
- ☐ Model and teach how to make text-to-text connections

OTHER

_____
_____
_____
_____
_____
_____
_____

Student Booklets

Assessments at Levels 28–40 include the use of Student Booklets. Each of these Benchmark Assessment Books has its own Student Booklet. This component of *DRA2, K–3*, gives students an opportunity to organize and write their thoughts about what they read. It supports the expectation that students think more deeply and critically about their reading and communicate their ideas in written form.

1 After reading a short passage from the text, students' responses to the Text Features and Prediction questions/prompts or the Prediction and Nonfiction Text Features questions/prompts are recorded by the teacher. Students write their own responses to the questions and prompts on the remaining pages.

Student Booklet · ***Missing Sneakers*** · Page 1

Name _____ Date _____

Teacher _____ Grade _____

The teacher reads aloud the prompts/questions and records the student's responses on this Before Reading page only.

BEFORE READING

TEXT FEATURES

Think about the title, the pictures you have seen, and what you have read so far. Tell me what you know about Sara and Sneakers.

1 Sara: _____

_____

Sneakers: _____

_____

_____

PREDICTION

What are 3 things you think might happen in the rest of this story?

1. _____

_____

Student Booklet · ***From Peanuts to Peanut Butter*** · Page 1

Name _____ Date _____

Teacher _____ Grade _____

The teacher reads aloud the prompts/questions and records the student's responses on this Before Reading page only.

BEFORE READING

PREDICTION

Open the book to the title and table of contents page. What are 3 questions you think may be answered as you read this book?

1. _____

_____

2. _____

_____

3. _____

1 _____

NONFICTION TEXT FEATURES

Turn to page 4. Why do you think the author put a heading at the top of this page?

_____

_____

Now read the map, and tell me what it shows you.

_____

_____

_____

From Peanuts to Peanut Butter

175

2 Independently, students read the remainder of the text and then write a summary of the important events and/or ideas.

AFTER READING

2 **Summary**

Write a summary of this story in your own words. Include the important characters, events, and details. You may use the book and the words below to help you write your summary.

In the beginning, _____

_____

_____

Next, _____

_____

_____

Then, _____

_____

_____

After that, _____

_____

_____

3 In order to demonstrate their understanding of what is explicitly stated in the text, students respond to the Literal Comprehension question(s) or prompt(s). They may compose their responses while looking at the texts.

3 **Literal Comprehension**

List 2 places where Sara looked for Sneakers.

Sara looked for Sneakers ...
1. _____
2. _____

4 Students interpret information inferred within the text and explain what in the text led them to their conclusions. Interpretation questions vary based on content and level.

4 **Interpretation**

What do you think Sara learned? _____

_____

_____

_____

5 Students reflect on what they read in order to determine what is most significant within the text or what they gained from their reading of the text. They also give a rationale for their decisions. Reflection questions vary based upon content and level.

5 **Reflection**

What do you think is the most important event in this story?

_____

_____

_____

Tell why you think it is important. _____

_____

_____

Reread what you have written to make sure your answers are the way you want them before you hand in your booklet.

6 At Level 40, students independently complete the Student Booklet. In addition to responding to Literal Comprehension, Interpretation, and Reflection questions, they are now asked to respond to Metacognitive awareness prompts. On page 4 of the Student Booklet, they select a comprehension strategy they used to construct and monitor their understanding while reading the text. They also cite examples in the text that demonstrate their use of the specific comprehension strategy.

It will generally take students 35 to 45 minutes to complete the Student Booklet portion of the assessment. The amount of time may vary depending upon the students' reading rates and time needed to formulate and record responses.

METACOGNITIVE AWARENESS

Check 1 strategy that you used to help you understand this text.

- ☐ I recalled what I know about the topic.
- ☐ I asked myself questions as I read.
- ☐ I made connections.
- ☐ I decided what was important to remember.
- ☐ I thought about the reasons why things happened.
- ☐ I pictured what was happening.

Give at least 2 specific examples from this book that show how you used this comprehension strategy.

6 _____

_____

_____

_____

_____

_____

Reread what you have written to make sure your answers are how you want them to be before you hand in your booklet.

Student Reading Survey

The *DRA2*, K–3, Student Reading Survey gives teachers an opportunity to assess students' level of Reading Engagement at Levels 28–40. It also encourages students to assume a greater responsibility in setting and achieving relevant reading goals. Students respond to questions in the following two areas:

- Wide Reading
- Self-Assessment/Goal Setting

If students use reading logs or other records of books read, they may refer to this list while completing the survey. This portion of the assessment may be administered individually, in small groups, or with the whole class. Most students will take approximately 15 minutes to complete the Student Reading Survey.

Note: Each student should attempt to write his or her own responses unless the student has an IEP or 504 Plan that requires the use of a scribe or other accommodations.

Grades K–3   *DRA2* Student Reading Survey   Page 1

Name _____ Date _____

Teacher _____ Grade _____

Complete the following sections to help you think about yourself as a reader.

Wide Reading

What books have you finished reading lately? You may use your record of books read.

1. _____
2. _____
3. _____
4. _____
5. _____
6. _____
7. _____

What are you reading at school now?

Grades K–3   *DRA2* Student Reading Survey   Page 2

Self-Assessment and Goal Setting

What are 3 things you do well as a reader?

1. _____
_____

2. _____
_____

3. _____
_____

What are 3 things you would like to work on to become a better reader?

1. _____
_____

2. _____
_____

3. _____
_____

315

Student Book Graph

The Student Book Graph reflects the increase in level of text difficulty read independently by students across their primary years. The shaded area represents below-grade-level performance. This graph also appears on the back cover of the Student Assessment Folder.

DRA2, *K–3*, Student Book Graph

DRA2 Stage	Grade	DRA2 Level		Name
Extending	Third Grade	40	Advanced / Independent / Instructional	
		38	Advanced / Independent / Instructional	
		34	Advanced / Independent / Instructional	
		30	Advanced / Independent / Instructional	
Transitional	Second Grade	28	Advanced / Independent / Instructional	
		24	Advanced / Independent / Instructional	
		20	Advanced / Independent / Instructional	
		18	Advanced / Independent / Instructional	
		16	Advanced / Independent / Instructional	
Early	First Grade	14	Advanced / Independent / Instructional	
		12	Advanced / Independent / Developing	
		10	Advanced / Independent / Developing	
		8	Advanced / Independent / Developing	
		6	Advanced / Independent / Developing	
		4	Advanced / Independent / Developing	
Emergent	Kindergarten	3	Independent / Developing	
		2	Independent / Developing	
		1	Developing	
		A	Developing	

Grade	Kindergarten	First	Second	Third
Assessment Dates				

Advanced: Total score for Oral Reading Fluency <u>and</u> Comprehension must be within the Advanced range on the Continuum.
Independent: Total score for Oral Reading Fluency <u>and</u> Comprehension must be at least within the Independent range on the Continuum.
Instructional: Total score for either Oral Reading Fluency or Comprehension is within the Instructional range on the Continuum.

308

Class Reporting Form

Use this form to record for school or district administrators students' *DRA2, K–3,* text levels and scores for Reading Engagement, Oral Reading Fluency, and Comprehension. If the assessment is used on a semi-annual basis, this form will also enable administrators and teachers to identify students who remain at risk in their development as readers.

Focus for Instruction: Class Profile

A variation of this form is available for each reading stage in *DRA2, K–3:* Emergent, Early, Transitional, and Extending. It enables you to decide how to group students for instruction based on specific needs. By checking the areas for instruction for each student, you will have information to assist you in planning for guided-reading lessons or whole-class lessons to facilitate growth in selected areas of Reading Engagement, Oral Reading Fluency, and/or Comprehension.

DRA2 Online Management System

DRA2 Online Management System users do not need to use this form, as the system will generate instructional groupings based on students' individual needs.

DRA2, K–3, Class Reporting Form

Teacher _____ School _____ Grade _____ Date _____

Names	Text Level (F/NF)	Reading Engagement Score	Oral Reading Fluency Score	Printed Language Concepts/ Comprehension Score

313

DRA2, K–3, Focus for Instruction: Class Profile for Transitional Readers

Levels 14–24

Grade Level _____ Date _____

Names	Text Level	Reading Engagement		Oral Reading Fluency			Comprehension					
		Book Selection	Sustained Reading	Expression and Phrasing	Rate	Accuracy: Word Analysis	Previewing/ Prediction	Retelling	Using Nonfiction Text Features	Reflection	Making Connections	Interpretation
1.												
2.												
3.												
4.												
5.												
6.												
7.												
8.												
9.												
10.												
11.												
12.												
13.												
14.												
15.												
16.												
17.												
18.												
19.												
20.												
21.												
22.												
23.												
24.												
25.												

Record students' names and check the areas selected as a focus for instruction. For students reading at Level 16, use **F** to indicate fiction and **NF** to indicate nonfiction next to the text level (e.g., 16F or 16NF).

311

Student Assessment Folder

The Student Assessment Folder provides storage and longitudinal monitoring of an individual student's progress. Each year, the Teacher Observation Guides, Student Reading Surveys (Levels 28–40), and Student Booklets (Levels 28–40) may be stored inside the folder.

1 The record of the student's *DRA2* levels shows how the student has progressed in recent years.

2 On the back of the Student Assessment Folder, the book graph documents the student's reading progress. The shaded area on the graph represents below-grade-level performance.

3 All assessment forms are stored in the left-side pocket for nonfiction and in the right-side pocket for fiction. The annual or semi-annual scores for specific categories are recorded.

DRA2 Online Management System

For *DRA2 Online Management System* users, the online *DRA2* reporting forms are used to record and report students' *DRA2* performance levels. The Student Assessment Folder can be used to store students' completed assessment papers.

**Developmental Reading Assessment®
K–3
Student Assessment Folder**

Name

Assessment Date	Grade	DRA2 Text Level	F or NF	DRA2 Grade-Level Performance		
				Below	On	Above

Front

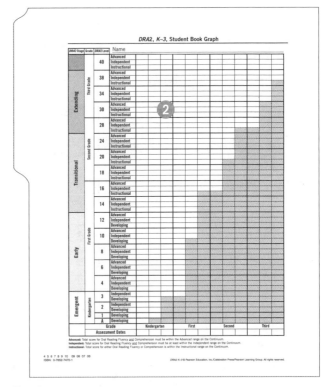

DRA2, K–3, Fiction Texts

Date	Benchmark Assessment Book Title	DRA2 Text Level	Accuracy	Reading Engagement	Oral Reading Fluency	Printed Language Concepts	Comprehension

Inside Right Pocket

Back

DRA2 K–3 Assessment Procedures Overview Card

Another new feature in *DRA2, K–3*, is the Assessment Procedures Overview reference card. This card summarizes the steps to follow in specific *DRA2*-level assessments. You will find a Record of Oral Reading Guidelines on the other side of the card. These guidelines show how to record various reading behaviors during students' oral reading. The guidelines are also provided on page 143 of this Teacher Guide.

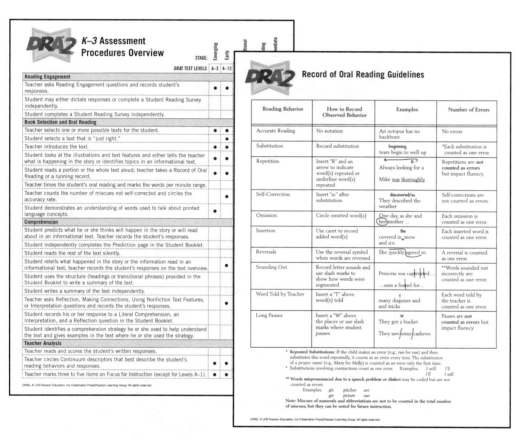

Training DVD

DRA2, K–3, includes a professional Training DVD, which teachers can use to learn how to administer the assessment or to review assessment procedures. Administrators or teacher trainers also can use the DVD in small training groups.

DRA Word Analysis

Also included with *DRA2, K–3*, is the *DRA Word Analysis*. This diagnostic assessment provides you with a systematic means to observe how struggling and emerging readers attend to and work with the various components of spoken and written words. The information you gather about students' knowledge and skills in working with words in context and in isolation will help you plan instruction for at-risk struggling and emerging readers.

The assessment consists of forty word-analysis tasks divided into five strands:

1. phonological awareness
2. metalanguage (language used to talk about printed language concepts)
3. letter/high-frequency word recognition
4. phonics
5. structural analysis and syllabication

Teachers are encouraged to use this separate assessment when more in-depth information is needed about students to help them attain reading proficiency. Note that the number of tasks students complete will vary based on their previous experiences, strengths, and needs.

DRA2 Online Management System

The *DRA2 Online Management System* (*DRA2 Online*) provides a powerful aid to teachers and districts using the *Developmental Reading Assessment K–3*, Second Edition. Like previous releases of *DRA Online*, Version 3.0 provides a secure environment for teachers to archive and manage student assessment results over time. Using *DRA2 Online*, you can do the following:

- **Archive student *DRA2* records online. All of the information collected from the Teacher Observation Guide, including the Continuum, and Focus for Instruction, for each student assessment is input into the system.**
- **Review student data that is calculated for you. Reading Engagement, Oral Reading Fluency, and Comprehension information is stored, compiled, and analyzed.**
- **Retrieve student data for a variety of purposes. Information is easily accessed and can be used to**
  - **Create instructional groups**
  - **Report individual student progress**
  - **Illustrate classroom, school, and district results**
  - **Determine the appropriate allocation for purchase of instructional materials**
  - **Create potential intervention or summer school groups**

In addition to the management of student data and reporting features, *DRA2 Online* also includes training on how to use the system and three User Guides for teachers, administrators (school and district), and report analysts. *DRA2 Online* customers will also have access online to the printable Blackline Masters assessment forms.

Technical Requirements: All users of the system must have a working email address. District and school email systems must also allow delivery of bulk email from Pearson. Java-enabled browsers, such as Microsoft® Internet Explorer™ 6.0 or Mozilla™ Firefox™ 1.0.6 for PCs or Microsoft Internet Explorer 5.2, Mozilla Firefox 1.0.3, or Apple® Safari™ 1.0.3 for Macintosh® computers are required, as well as access to secure Web sites. PCs also require Macromedia® Flash™ Player 7.

To find out more about the *DRA2 Online Management System*, email DRA.Pearson@pearsonschool.com. To see *DRA2 Online* in action, take a tour: www.pearsonschool.com/dratour.

DRA2 Online Writer

With the *DRA2 Online Management System* users have the option of purchasing separately a *DRA2 Online Writer*, powered by Anoto®. The pen records teacher writing on specially printed Teacher Observation Guides. When an assessment is completed, the pen is returned to its holder, and the data is automatically uploaded to the *DRA2 Online Management System*, bypassing the need to type assessment information into a computer.

DRA2 Organizer

Your *DRA2, K–3,* box is also a handy organizer. The organizer has been updated and includes separate hanging file folders that make storing each assessment text and its associated forms easy.

DRA2 Clipboard

New to *DRA2, K–3,* is the *DRA2* Clipboard. This tool provides a clock, timer, and calculator, as well as a handy writing surface to use during individual assessment conferences. The absence of an obvious and distinct timer may help to prevent student assessment anxiety.

Conference Formats/Comparable Books

At the heart of *DRA2* is the one-on-one conference. Such conferences permit you to observe and interact with students as you record their responses and observable reading behaviors. The information gathered enables you to

- determine a reader's independent *DRA2* level
- confirm or redirect ongoing instruction
- group students effectively for reading experiences and instruction
- document changes over time in reading performance
- identify students who may be working below proficiency and who need further assessment (e.g., *DRA Word Analysis*) or intervention

The format for *DRA2* conferences changes over time to honor and support what readers can do as they move toward independence. Following is a description of a conference format for different ranges of text levels. Also listed are a variety of books that are comparable to the *DRA* text levels and their approximate grade levels. These books were sorted by common characteristics and leveled by classroom teachers. Thinking about where and what a student is reading on a daily basis and locating similar books on the list should give you a general sense of which book(s) to select for the *DRA2* conference. Nonfiction *DRA2* texts have been marked with an asterisk.

After the conference, you may use the list once again to think about what types and levels of books the student is ready to read next. Please refer also to Pearson Learning Group's publication *Matching Children With Books* for an extensive list of DRA-leveled student books available for use in the classroom.

DRA2, Levels A–3

Students who are reading Levels A–3 need a great deal of support. Select the appropriate Benchmark Assessment Book, prompt students as needed during the preview, and read one or more pages to introduce the text pattern before asking students to read. The Benchmark Assessment Books and comparable book titles are as follows:

DRA2 Leveled Texts		Comparable Titles
A	*Can You Sing?*	*Oops!* (Little Celebrations/Pearson Learning Group)
1	*Things That Go* *What Is Red?*	*The Bath* (Ready Readers/Pearson Learning Group) *My Book* (Maris/Viking) *Two* (Little Celebrations/Pearson Learning Group)
2	*I Can See* *Bath Time*	*Have You Seen My Cat?* (Carle/Putnam) *Have You Seen My Duckling?* (Tafuri/Greenwillow)
3	*The "I Like" Game* *Look at Me*	*An Elephant's Trunk* (Little Celebrations/Pearson Learning) *Potatoes on Tuesday* (Little Celebrations/Pearson Learning)

DRA2, Levels 4–12

Students who are reading Levels 4–12 may be asked to choose a Benchmark Assessment Book that seems just right from a range of three texts. Use suggested prompts as needed to scaffold these readers as they preview the story, give a retelling, and respond to the text. The Benchmark Assessment Books and comparable book titles are as follows:

DRA2 Leveled Texts		Comparable Titles
4	Get Your Umbrella Where Is My Hat?	Brown Bear, Brown Bear (Martin/Holt) Baby Says (Steptoe/Morrow) Flying (Crews/Mulberry Books)
6	Time to Play Why Are We Stopping?	How Many Bugs in a Box? (Carter/Simon & Schuster) The Ball Bounced (Tafuri/Morrow) Bears on Wheels (Berenstain/Random House)
8	Duke The Lost Book	Go, Dog, Go! (Eastman/Random House) All By Myself (Mayer/Golden) Henry's Busy Day (Campbell/The Penguin Group)
10	Grandma's Surprise Shoe Boxes	Just Like Daddy (Asch/Simon & Schuster) The Old Oak Tree (Little Celebrations/Pearson Learning) Dear Zoo (Campbell/Macmillan)
12	Allie's Wish Robert's New Friend	Gone Fishing (Long/Houghton Mifflin) Titch (Hutchins/Penguin) Nicky Upstairs and Downstairs (Ziefert/Penguin Group)

DRA2, Levels 14–16

Begin to time student's oral reading beginning with Level 14 texts. The conference format for these texts is the same as for DRA2, Levels 4–12. The Benchmark Assessment Books and comparable book titles are as follows:

DRA2 Leveled Texts		Comparable Titles
14	A New School The Wagon	Clean House for Mole and Mouse (Ziefert/Scholastic) You'll Soon Grow into Them, Titch (Hutchins/Morrow) Just Me and My Dad (Mayer/Donovon)
16	Animal Homes* Baby Birds* Chip to the Rescue Monkey's Stepping Stones	Are You My Mother? (Eastman/Random House) Fix-It (McPhail/Penguin) Hattie and the Fox (Fox/Bradbury/Trumpet) Paper Wasps (Little Celebrations/Pearson Learning) Follow a River (iOpeners/Pearson Learning)

*Nonfiction Texts

DRA2, Levels 18–24

Students reading Benchmark Assessment Books Levels 18–24 read the opening section aloud while the teacher takes a record of oral reading. If the student meets the oral reading criteria, the student finishes reading the story independently and then completes the conference with an oral retelling and response. Note: It should take students approximately 8 minutes or less to read the text silently. The Benchmark Assessment Books and comparable book titles are as follows:

DRA2 Leveled Texts		Comparable Titles
18	*Game Day* *A Giant in the Forest*	*Little Bear* (Minarik/ Harper Collins) *There's Something in My Attic* (Mayer/Penguin Group)
20	*Green Freddie* *Turtle's Big Race*	*Henry and Mudge* (Rylant/Aladdin) *Frog and Toad* (Lobel/Harper & Row)
24	*Thin as a Stick* *The Wonderful Day*	*Arthur* books (Hoban/Harper Collins) *Nate the Great* (Weinman/Dell)

DRA2, Levels 28–38

Students reading Benchmark Assessment Books Levels 28–38 respond to questions on a Student Reading Survey, read a complete story independently, and respond in writing to specific questions in a Student Booklet. Independent reading should take approximately 8 to 18 minutes, depending upon the length of the text. The Benchmark Assessment Books and comparable book titles are as follows:

DRA2 Leveled Texts		Comparable Titles
28	*Animals Can Help** *From Peanuts to Peanut Butter** *Missing Sneakers* *You Don't Look Beautiful to Me*	*All About Stacy* (Giff/Dell) *The Stories Julian Tells* (Cameron/Random House) *On the Farm* (iOpeners/Pearson Learning Group) *Undersea Gardens* (iOpeners/Pearson Learning Group)
30	*Busy Helpers* *Tiger's Whirlwind Day*	*Cam Jensen* (Adler/Puffin Books) *Peewee Scouts* series (Delton/Dell)
34	*The Mystery at the Mays' House* *Summer Discovery*	*Lake Critter Journal* (Little Celebrations/Pearson Learning Group) *The Hit Away Kid* (Christopher/Dell)
38	*Mae Jemison: Shooting for the Stars** *Slammin' Sammy: A Real Hero** *A Trip Through Time* *Trouble at the Beaver Pond*	*Shark in School* (Giff/Dell) *Box Car Children* (Warner/Albert Whitman) *Astronauts Take Flight* (iOpeners/Pearson Learning Group) *All About Bikes* (iOpeners/Pearson Learning Group)

*Nonfiction Texts

DRA2, Level 40

The Level 40 texts are a part of *DRA2, 4–8*. They are included in *DRA2, K–3*, to be used with third-grade students who are reading above grade level. Students complete a Student Reading Survey and Student Booklet independently. The independent reading should take approximately 20 minutes or less. The Benchmark Assessment Books and comparable book titles are as follows:

DRA2 Leveled Texts		Comparable Titles
40	*A Pack of Wolves** *The Amazing Octopus** *All the Way Under* *A Journey to Freedom*	*The Magic School Bus* series (Cole/Scholastic) *Little House on the Prairie* (Wilder/Harper Collins) *Amazing Arachnids* (Floyd/Pearson Learning Group) *Saving the Florida Panther* (Otfinoski/Pearson Learning Group)

*Nonfiction Texts

Developmental Reading Assessment Guidelines

Once you begin to implement *DRA2* in your classroom, you will find an organizational system that works well for you. After a while, you will know just what to do, observe, record on the forms, and circle on the Continuum. Most teachers report that after four or five assessments, *DRA2* is much easier to use. Eventually you will find yourself automatically analyzing student responses each time you interact with them as readers. Using the information gained from the *DRA2* to select several Focuses for Instruction will help you become aware of what individuals or groups of students need to learn, practice, and extend.

The *DRA2, K–3,* Training DVD also supports the use of *DRA2.* Viewing the different conference formats will help you understand how the conferences and students' responses vary over time. It is recommended that you view the DVD with colleagues. Opportunities to discuss your observations and perceptions of developing readers with others will enable you to confirm your judgments or alter your opinions and establish expectations.

Preparing for the Assessment

STEP 1 Check to see that you have the books and forms you need to conduct the assessments.

The *DRA2, K–3,* kit includes

- Teacher Guide
- Benchmark Assessment Books (Levels A to 40)

The following forms can be found in the Blackline Masters book or on the Blackline Masters CD:

- an assessment Teacher Observation Guide for each text, which includes the Record of Oral Reading, the Continuum, and the Focus for Instruction
- Student Booklets for text Levels 28–40

- Student Reading Survey for students reading text Levels 28–40
- Student Book Graph
- Student Assessment Form
- Focus for Instruction: Class Profile for each reading stage
- Class Reporting Form

STEP 2 Make copies of the assessment forms you plan to use for each student.

You will need

- Teacher Observation Guides
- Student Booklets (Levels 28–40)
- Student Reading Surveys (Levels 28–40)

STEP 3 Assemble assessment materials.

Organize the Teacher Observation Guides, Student Booklets, and Benchmark Assessment Books by level for easy access and storage. The *DRA2* organizer with leveled hanging file folders is included for this purpose. A folder is provided for each title.

STEP 4 Review or learn how to take and analyze a running record or a record of oral reading.

Directions for taking a running record appear in *An Observation of Early Literacy Achievement* by Marie Clay and *Guided Reading: Good First Teaching for All Children* by Irene Fountas and Gay Su Pinnell. Directions for taking a record of oral reading appear in the back of this guide and on the laminated Assessment Procedures Overview card.

STEP 5 Read all the Benchmark Assessment Books that you will be using.

It is important for you to know the texts that your students read in order to support and evaluate students' retellings and determine levels of comprehension.

STEP 6 Prepare an assessment timeline and activities for the other students.

Generally teachers find they can comfortably assess two children a day, so the assessment window should be set for two to three weeks. You may wish to plan for more time if you feel you will not be able to assess two children every day. You will want to select a time each day for the assessment conferences when other students are engaged in quiet activities that they can self-sustain. You may begin with your students who are emerging, early, or struggling readers so that you have the needed information to plan their instruction more effectively. If you choose, you may begin with your better, more competent readers. While a student reading Level 18 and above reads silently, you may begin another *DRA2* conference or interact with other students. Each time you administer the assessment, you will become more comfortable with the procedures.

STEP 7 Prepare students for DRA2.

As part of ongoing classroom instruction, model and have students reading at Level 4 and higher practice retelling familiar stories. Begin modeling and providing opportunities for students reading above Level 28 to construct written responses for texts they are currently reading.

Note: There are generic *DRA2* Blackline Masters on pages 130–139 for students to use with texts other than *DRA2* Benchmark Assessment Books.

In preparation for the assessment, share with students what each will be asked to do during the conference. You will also want to discuss what is expected of the other students while conferences are being conducted.

STEP 8 Select and prepare a place for the assessment conference.

The assessment area should be quiet and free from major distractions but should allow you to see the rest of the class. Generally, a small table where you can sit beside the child is sufficient. Assessment materials, pen or pencil, stopwatch and calculator for Levels 14–40 (the clipboard that comes with the *DRA2* kit has a stopwatch and a calculator built in), and a tape recorder should be within easy reach. Audiotaping student conferences is an option that permits you to listen a second time if needed. The audiotape is also an additional means of documenting change in student oral reading achievement over time.

Classroom Management Tips

Many teachers have asked for advice on how to manage the classroom during the assessment. Suggestions from teachers who have developed a successful system for conducting the assessment are listed below.

1. Assess two students a day over two weeks during a Readers Workshop or during a reading period. You could also conduct assessments during times when students are at different centers within the classroom or engaged in other meaningful activities that they can sustain independently. While the assessment may take away some instruction time over the two- or three-week period, it is really the only way to ensure that reading instruction is properly tailored to students' needs. Assessment is also some of the most important work you will do over the course of the year.

2. Consider working with a colleague to complete the assessments. You provide instruction and supervision for both classes one day while your colleague conducts the assessment with his or her students. A few days later, switch roles and have your colleague provide the supervision and instruction while you conduct the assessment with your own students.

3. Your school could hire a substitute teacher to provide instruction while you administer the assessment. With one day dedicated to assessment, teachers are often able to pull out and assess the majority of their students during this time.

However you choose to manage your classroom during the assessment, remember that you should be the one actually administering the assessment to your students. Doing so ensures that you'll gain valuable information on which to base your teaching.

Plan to give the assessment in a quiet part of your room that will allow you to closely observe and quietly converse with each student with no major distractions or interruptions. It is important that stories being read aloud or retold not be overheard by other students.

The following chart provides an overview of the different *DRA2, K–3,* conference procedures.

	Stage:	Emerging	Early	Transitional		Extending	Intermediate
DRA2, K–3, Conference Formats for DRA2 Text Levels		A–3	4–12	14–16	18–24	28–38	40
1. Reading Engagement							
Teacher asks Reading Engagement questions and records student's responses.		●	●	●	●		
Student may either dictate responses or complete a Student Reading Survey and self-assessment independently.						●	
Student completes a Student Reading Survey independently.							●
2. Book Selection and Oral Reading							
Teacher selects one or more possible texts for the student.		●	●	●	●	●	●
Student selects a text that is "just right."			●	●	●	●	●
Teacher introduces the text.		●	●	●	●	●	●
Student looks at the illustrations and text features and either tells the teacher what is happening in the story or identifies topics in an informational text.		●	●	●			
Student reads a portion or the whole text aloud; teacher takes a Record of Oral Reading or a running record and determines accuracy and fluency.		●	●	●	●	●	●
Student demonstrates an understanding of words used to talk about printed language and demonstrates an understanding of concepts of print.		●					
Teacher times the student's oral reading.				●	●	●	●
3. Comprehension							
Student predicts what he or she thinks will happen in the story or will read about in an informational text. Teacher records the student's responses.					●	●	
Student independently completes the Prediction page in the Student Booklet.							●
Student reads the rest of the text silently.					●	●	●
Student retells what happened in the story or the information read in an informational text; teacher records the student's responses on the text overview.			●	●	●		
Student uses the structure (headings or transitional phrases) provided in the Student Booklet to write a summary of the text.						●	
Student writes a summary of the text independently.							●
Teacher asks Reflection, Making Connections, Using Nonfiction Text Features, or Interpretation questions and records the student's responses.			●	●	●		
Student records his or her response to a Literal Comprehension, an Interpretation, and a Reflection question in the Student Booklet.						●	●
Student identifies a comprehension strategy he or she used to help understand the text and gives examples in the text where he or she used the strategy.							●

Conducting the Assessment Conference

STEP 1 Select a range of leveled texts.

For the purpose of this assessment, it is important that students select a text that is "just right" for them so their attention can be focused primarily on constructing meaning and not so much on decoding. Use previous *DRA2* or other reading assessment information to determine the highest text levels you believe the student can read independently.

- If the student is obviously an Emergent reader, then begin with Level A.

- If the student's *DRA2* record indicates that he or she read and responded at an Independent level of performance on his/her last *DRA2*, then select an appropriate range of texts based on the student's current reading material.

- If giving *DRA2* for the first time in the beginning of the school year, use the chart below. It suggests which *DRA2* text levels to select based on the student's current grade and previous year's level of reading performance.

- If giving the *DRA2* for the first time at either the middle or end of year, select an initial *DRA2* text based on your knowledge of that student's performance in guided reading groups, individual reading conferences, or information from his/her previous school to help narrow the range of possible texts. You may use the list of comparable books in this guide on pages 37–39 or refer to *Matching Children With Books* from Pearson Learning Group to assist in selecting an appropriate range of *DRA2* text levels.

STEP 2 Have the student select a text.

Invite the student to select a text that seems "just right" (not too hard or too easy) from the range of texts you selected for the assessment. Follow the directions on the Teacher Observation Guide for the selected text. If the selected text is obviously too difficult, politely stop the reading and then select and introduce a lower level text.

Follow the directions on the Teacher Observation Guide for the text selected. Note that the directions change from level to level.

Student's Current Grade	If the student's level of reading performance was ...	Select a text from the following *DRA2* Level(s) at the beginning of the year
Kindergarten	not applicable	Optional for teacher
First Grade	on grade level in kindergarten	3–4
	below grade level in kindergarten	A–2
	above grade level in kindergarten	8–14
Second Grade	on grade level in 1st grade	16–18
	below grade level in 1st grade	10–14
	above grade level in 1st grade	28*–34
Third Grade	on grade level in 2nd grade	28–30
	below grade level in 2nd grade	18–24
	above grade level in 2nd grade	34–38*

Note: It is important that you make sure students are able to read/decode and comprehend both nonfiction and fiction texts on their present grade level before asking them to read an above-grade-level text.

Assessment Guidelines

STEP 3 Record the student's responses and behaviors in each of the following areas.

Reading Engagement

Levels A–24

1 Briefly jot down the student's responses to each of the preference questions on the Teacher Observation Guide.

Levels 28–38

Students may either dictate their responses or complete the Student Reading Survey independently prior to the assessment.

Oral Reading Fluency

Introduction and Preview

Levels 1–3

If the student is unable to name half of the items pictured in the text, use your best judgment to decide whether you should continue with the assessment.

Levels 4–16

2 Note the student's use of connecting words (*and*, *then*, *but*) and vocabulary relevant to the text. You may use general prompts, such as "Now what is happening?" or "Turn the page," but do not ask specific questions.

Teacher Observation Guide · *Duke* · Level 8, Page 1

Name/Date __Gillian__ · Teacher/Grade __1ˢᵗ__

Scores: Reading Engagement _5_/8 · Oral Reading Fluency _13_/16 · Comprehension _22_/28
Independent Range: 6–7 · 11–14 · 19–25

Book Selection · Text selected by: ☐ teacher · ☒ student

1. READING ENGAGEMENT

(If the student has recently answered these questions, skip this section.)

1 *Tell me about one of your favorite books.* __Brown Mouse Plays a Trick__
__He plays a trick on the cat.__

T: Do you like to read ☐ alone, ☒ with a buddy, or ☐ with a group?

Why? __It fun - we take turns__

T: Whom do you read with at home? __my mom and sister__

2. ORAL READING FLUENCY

INTRODUCTION AND PREVIEW

T: In this story, Duke, *a boy named Jim has a black-and-white dog named Duke. Duke can do lots of tricks. Look at the pictures, and tell me what is happening in this story.*

__Duke, jump over, throw, lick__

2 te the student's use of connecting words (e.g., *and, then, but*) and vocabulary relevant to the text. You may use general prompts, such as "Now what is happening?" or "Turn the page," but do not ask specific questions. Tally the number of times you prompt. __and then__

RECORD OF ORAL READING

Record the student's oral reading behaviors on the Record of Oral Reading below and on the following page.

T: Duke. *Now, read to find out what Duke can do.*

Page 2

Jim had a dog. The dog was black and white. The dog's name was Duke.

Page 3

Duke was a big dog. He had big feet. Jim liked his dog. __him (sc)__

Duke **8**

45

45

Record of Oral Reading

Levels A–40

3 Record the student's oral reading behaviors (e.g., miscues, substitutions, rereading, sounding out, self-corrections) on the Record of Oral Reading.

Levels 14–40

4 For these levels, time the student's oral reading. Note the reader's phrasing, expression, and attention to punctuation, as well as what happens at difficulty and with miscues. As students become Extending readers, processing strategies occur in the head most of the time and are not observable. It may be helpful to tape-record the student's oral reading and to listen to the audiotape after the conference.

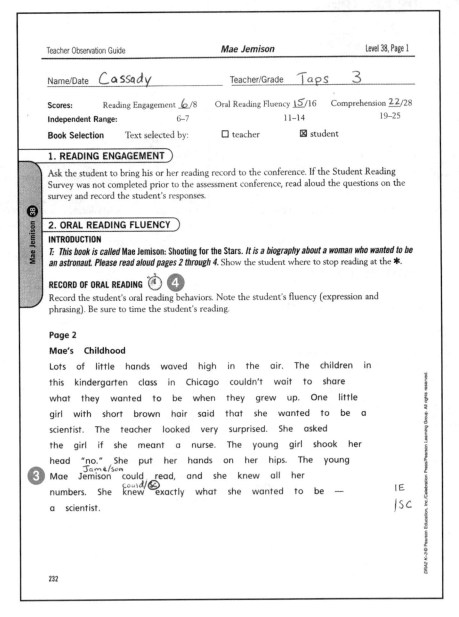

Teacher Observation Guide   *Mae Jemison*   Level 38, Page 1

Name/Date *Cassady*   Teacher/Grade *Taps 3*

Scores: Reading Engagement **6**/8   Oral Reading Fluency **15**/16   Comprehension **22**/28
Independent Range: 6–7   11–14   19–25

Book Selection   Text selected by: ☐ teacher   ☒ student

Mae Jemison 38

1. READING ENGAGEMENT

Ask the student to bring his or her reading record to the conference. If the Student Reading Survey was not completed prior to the assessment conference, read aloud the questions on the survey and record the student's responses.

2. ORAL READING FLUENCY

INTRODUCTION

T: *This book is called* Mae Jemison: Shooting for the Stars. *It is a biography about a woman who wanted to be an astronaut. Please read aloud pages 2 through 4.* Show the student where to stop reading at the ✱.

RECORD OF ORAL READING ⏱ **4**

Record the student's oral reading behaviors. Note the student's fluency (expression and phrasing). Be sure to time the student's reading.

Page 2

Mae's   Childhood

Lots   of   little   hands   waved   high   in   the   air.   The   children   in
this   kindergarten   class   in   Chicago   couldn't   wait   to   share
what   they   wanted   to   be   when   they   grew   up.   One   little
girl   with   short   brown   hair   said   that   she   wanted   to   be   a
scientist.   The   teacher   looked   very   surprised.   She   asked
the   girl   if   she   meant   a   nurse.   The   young   girl   shook   her
head   "no."   She   put   her   hands   on   her   hips.   The   young
3 Mae   Jemison   [Jame/son]   could   read,   and   she   knew   all   her
numbers.   She   knew   [could/SC]   exactly   what   she   wanted   to   be —   IE
a   scientist.   /SC

232

⑤ Record the student's time.

⑥ As soon as the student finishes reading orally, quickly count the number of miscues that are not self-corrected. Circle the appropriate box on the Oral Reading Percent of Accuracy chart.

⑦ For Levels 14–40, after you time the oral reading, use the Words Per Minute chart to identify the WPM range.

⑧ Stop the assessment if the student's score falls in the shaded areas (below the Independent level) for either words-per-minute or accuracy. Reassess the student with a lower-level text immediately or at another time.

Teacher Observation Guide   *Mae Jemison*   Level 38, Page 2

Page 3

Mae Jemison was born in Alabama in 1956. She was the youngest of ^the three children. Her family moved to Chicago, Illinois, when she was three years old. From the time she was a young girl, Mae worked hard. She was an excellent student.   IE

Mae loved visiting the library. It was just a mile from her house. She read all sorts of books about space. By the time she was ten years old, Mae knew she would travel in space someday.

Page 4

Mae as a Young Woman

When she was sixteen years old, Mae finished high school. She went to college. She earned two **degrees.** Then she went to medical school to become a doctor.

⑤ Time: _1:29_ minutes:seconds

ORAL READING WORDS PER MINUTE, PERCENT OF ACCURACY

Use the student's oral reading time to circle the WPM range.

Word Count: 210

	INTRVN	INSTR	IND	ADV
Minutes:Seconds	3:02 or more	3:01–2:21	2:20–1:41	1:40 or less
WPM	69 or less	70–89	90–125	126 or more

Count the number of miscues that are not self-corrected. Circle the percent of accuracy based on the number of miscues.

	INTRVN	INSTR	IND			ADV	
Number of Miscues	12 or more	10–11	8–9	6–7	4–5	1–3	0
Percent of Accuracy	94 or less	95	96	97	98	99	100

⑧ • If the student's score falls in a shaded area for either WPM or Accuracy, STOP! Reassess with a lower level text at another time.

233

Assessment Guidelines

47

Comprehension: Prediction

Oral Predictions

Levels 18–24

9 Note and count the number of possible events or actions that students predict.

Note: Students do not use the text when making their predictions.

Levels 28–38

10 Read aloud the questions/prompts on page 1 in the Student Booklet, and record the student's responses on the same page. Do not give additional prompts.

Note: Students may use the book when responding to the Text Features prompts and nonfiction Prediction prompt, but the book should be *closed* when they make their predictions for fiction books.

Teacher Observation Guide   *A Giant in the Forest*   Level 18, Page 3

A Giant in the Forest 18

3. COMPREHENSION

PREDICTION

Students do not use the text when making their predictions. Record the student's responses. **9**

T: **Think about the title, the pictures you have seen, and what you have read so far.** (Pause) **Tell me three things that you think might happen in the rest of this story.**

SILENT READING

T: **Now, it's time to read and enjoy this story by yourself. When you are done, please come to me and I'll ask you to tell me what happened in this story.**

RETELLING

As the student retells, underline and record on the Story Overview the information included in the student's retelling. Please note the student does not need to use the exact words.

T: Close the book before the retelling, and then say: **Start at the beginning, and tell me what happened in this story.**

Story Overview
Beginning
1. A little boy lived next to a forest with a lake.
2. A big, ugly giant lived in the forest. He slept all day but walked in the forest at night looking for things to eat.
3. Mother sent the boy to the lake to take a bath.
4. She told the boy, "You'll be safe in the lake because the giant can't swim. Be home before dark."
Middle
5. On his way to the lake to take a bath, the boy found a baby bird on the ground and put it back in its nest.
6. Mother bird sang—and the boy sat down and listened.
7. It was getting dark when he got to the lake. He took a bath as fast as he could.
8. The boy started home after dark. He saw the giant.
9. The boy ran back to the lake, dropped his soap and . . .
End

Student Booklet   *Mae Jemison*   Page 1

Name   Cassady   Date   7/7/05

Teacher   Taps   Grade   3

The teacher reads aloud the prompts/questions and records the student's responses on this Before Reading page only.

BEFORE READING

TEXT FEATURES

PREDICTION

Open the book to the title and table of contents page. What are 3 questions you think may be answered as you read this book? **10**

1. Could not respond.

2. _____

3. _____

NONFICTION TEXT FEATURES

Turn to page 4. Read the map and tell me what this map shows you.

Countries Mae visited as a young doctor - Cuba, Sierra Leone, Liberia, Kenya and Thailand.

Turn to the glossary. What does the word *degrees* mean in this book?

Certificates given to students who have completed advanced training or education.

Mae Jemison

238

Written Predictions

Level 40

11 If it will help students, you may read aloud the prompts/questions on the Prediction page before they complete their predictions independently, but do not give additional prompts.

*Note: Students are not to use the book to complete the Prediction page.

Student Booklet   *A Pack of Wolves*   Page 1

Name _Casey_   Date _May 19, 2004_

Teacher _Mrs. Jones_   Grade _3_

BEFORE READING

PREDICTION

11 What questions did you have as you were reading the first part of this text?

1. _Why are their eyes yellow?_

2. _How long are their tails?_

3. _How do they hunt?_

What do you think you will learn from reading the rest of this text?

1. _How they hunt their meals._

2. _Why their ears are pointed._

3. _Why they howl._

Let your teacher know when you have completed this page.

301

A Pack of Wolves

Assessment Guidelines

Comprehension: Oral and Written

Reading that is truly satisfying and effective is meaning-driven. When students are frequently asked to "read" texts they do not understand, reading becomes a meaningless task that carries little value for them. Therefore, it is important to take the time to listen carefully as students respond orally or to analyze written responses to determine whether they truly understand what they are reading.

For the sake of time, you may be tempted to shorten the assessment. For example, you may decide to simply take a record of oral reading to determine a student's rate of accuracy. If this is the case, remember that accuracy rate is just one factor in determining a student's independent text level.

Oral Retelling

Levels 4–24

1. As the student retells, underline and record the information included in the Story Overview on the Teacher Observation Guide. Please note the student does not need to use the exact words in order for you to underline the statement. Tally the number of times you prompted the student.

2. If necessary, use one or more of the suggested prompts to gain further information after the initial retelling. Prompting should continue until you believe the student has shared all that he or she can remember from the text. Do not ask other questions.

A *DRA2* Benchmark Assessment Book is considered to be at an Independent level for a student only when the student's total scores for Oral Reading Fluency and Comprehension are at least within the Independent range on the Continuum.

Some students will read a text with a high rate of accuracy and fluency. These students appear to be proficient readers, but their oral or written responses will confirm what they actually understood and recalled about the text. Therefore, administer the complete assessment.

Teacher Observation Guide   *Duke*   Level 8, Page 3

3. COMPREHENSION

RETELLING

As the student retells, underline and record on the Story Overview the information included in the student's retelling. Please note the student does not need to use the exact words.

T: Close the book, and then say: **Start at the beginning, and tell me what happened in this story.**

Story Overview

Beginning

1. Jim has a black and white dog with big feet named Duke.
2. Duke likes to play with Jim, and he can do lots of tricks. *(dog)*

Middle

3. Duke sits up and shakes hands, and Jim says, "Good dog!" *(He) (with)*

TP 4. Duke jumps over a stick, and Jim says, "Good dog!" *(He)*

TP 5. Duke gets the ball, and Jim says, "Good dog!"

End

TP⑤ 6. Duke likes to lick Jim's face. Duke is a good dog.

If the retelling is limited, use one or more of the following prompts to gain further information. Place a checkmark by a prompt each time it is used.

2. ☑ *Tell me more.*
   ☐ *What happened at the beginning?*
   ☐ *What happened before/after* _____ (an event mentioned by the student)?
   ☐ *Who else was in the story?*
   ☑ *How did the story end?*

REFLECTION

Record the student's responses to the prompts and questions below.

T: **What part did you like best in this story? Tell me why you liked that part.** *I liked it when he shook hands. Because my dog shakes hands with me.*

MAKING CONNECTIONS

Note: If the student makes a text-to-self connection in his or her response to the above prompt, skip the following question.

T: **What did this story make you think of?** or **What connections did you make while reading this story?** *my dog Max – he does tricks but my dad sold him.*

Duke ⑧

47

STEP 3 continued...

Oral Responses

Levels 4–16

3 Record student responses to the Reflection and Making Connections questions/prompts.

Levels 18–24

At these levels, students will give oral responses to Reflection and Interpretation questions/prompts.

---

3. COMPREHENSION

RETELLING

As the student retells, underline and record on the Story Overview the information included in the student's retelling. Please note the student does not need to use the exact words.

T: Close the book, and then say: ***Start at the beginning, and tell me what happened in this story.***

Story Overview
Beginning
✓1. Jim has a <u>black and white dog</u> with big feet named <u>Duke</u>.
✓2. <u>Duke likes to play with Jim</u>, and he can do lots of <u>tricks</u>.
Middle
✓3. Duke sits up and shakes hands, and Jim says, "Good dog!"
TP 4. Duke jumps over a <u>stick</u>, and Jim says, "Good dog!"
TP 5. Duke gets the ball, and Jim says, "Good dog!"
End
TP Ⓢ 6. <u>Duke likes to lick Jim's face</u>. Duke is a good dog.

If the retelling is limited, use one or more of the following prompts to gain further information. Place a checkmark by a prompt each time it is used.

☑ *Tell me more.*
☐ *What happened at the beginning?*
☐ *What happened before/after* _____ (an event mentioned by the student)*?*
☐ *Who else was in the story?*
☑ *How did the story end?*

REFLECTION

Record the student's responses to the prompts and questions below.

T: ***What part did you like best in this story? Tell me why you liked that part.***
I liked it when he shook hands. Because my dog shakes hands with me.

MAKING CONNECTIONS

Note: If the student makes a text-to-self connection in his or her response to the above prompt, skip the following question.

T: ***What did this story make you think of?*** or ***What connections did you make while reading this story?***
my dog Max – he does tricks but my dad sold him.

Duke **8**

Assessment Guidelines

Written Summary and Responses

Levels 28–40

For Extending and Intermediate Readers you may read aloud the questions/prompts in the Student Booklet before the student begins if that will help the student. Do not give additional prompts or suggestions.

Student Booklet   *Mae Jemison*   Page 2

AFTER READING

SUMMARY

Write a summary of this book in your own words. Include the important ideas and facts. You may use the book and the headings below to help you write your summary.

Mae's Childhood Mae wanted to be a scientist. She was born in 1956 in Alabama.

Mae as a Young Woman In college Mae earned 2 degrees. When she was 16 she went to medical school to become a doctor.

Mae's Space Training In 1987 Mae was picked become a astronaut. Before she go in space she lernd about the shuttle.

Mae's First Flight in Space Mae was the first African American women to travl space. She went with 6 other people.

In the Spacelab When she went to space a hurricane and chicago. In space watched how tadpoles became frog space.

A Dream Come True Mae was in space for 8 She flew more than 3 million miles space.

Student Booklet   *Mae Jemison*   Page 3

LITERAL COMPREHENSION

List 3 things that Mae learned to do in the astronaut training program.

Mae learned...
1. How to use the space shuttle.
2. What it was like in space.
3. What the suit did.

INTERPRETATION

Why do you think Mae wanted to be an astronaut? Because she was instrid in space scienece.

REFLECTION

What do you think is the most important thing that you learned from this book?

That you can be anything that you want to be when you grow up.

Tell why you think it is important. Because back then not all women could be anything they wanted.

Reread what you have written to make sure your answers are the way you want them before you hand in your booklet.

240

52

Analyzing Student Performance

After you have completed the conference, the next step is to analyze the student's responses and the notes you made on the assessment form(s). The following chart provides an overview of what the teacher analyzes after completing the *DRA2* conference:

Stage:	Emerging	Early	Transitional		Extending	Interme-diate
Teacher Analysis and Evaluation	A–3	4–12	14–16	18–24	28–38	40
Teacher analyzes the student's oral reading behaviors to determine rate of accuracy, types of miscues, and problem-solving strategies.	●	●	●	●	●	●
Teacher analyzes the student's WPM (starts at Level 14).			●	●	●	●
Teacher analyzes the student's responses to prompts about concepts of print and words used to talk about printed language.	●					
Teacher records and analyzes the student's oral responses to determine a level of comprehension.		●	●	●		
Teacher reads and analyzes the student's written responses to determine level of comprehension.					●	●

STEP 1 After the DRA2 conference, complete the Teacher Observation Guide.

1 Use the information on the Record of Oral Reading to check the appropriate responses on the Analysis of Oral Reading chart.

Levels 14–40

2 To calculate the student's fluency rate, convert the student's oral reading time to all seconds. Then use the formula to calculate the student's exact WPM.

Teacher Observation Guide | *Mae Jemison* | Level 38, Page 4

4. TEACHER ANALYSIS

ORAL READING

If the student had 5 or more different miscues, use the information recorded on the Record of Oral Reading to complete the chart below.

Student problem-solves words using:	
☐ beginning letter(s)/sound(s)	Number of miscues self-corrected: __1__
☐ letter-sound clusters	Number of miscues not self-corrected: __2__ **1**
☐ blending letters/sounds	Number of words told to the student: __0__

Miscues interfered with meaning:	Miscues included:
☐ onset and rime	
☐ knowledge of spelling patterns (analogies)	☐ never / ☐ omissions
☐ syllables	☐ at times / ☐ insertions
☐ rereading	☐ often / ☐ reversals
☐ no observable behaviors	☐ substitutions that were
	☐ visually similar
	☐ not visually similar

Copy each substitution to help analyze the student's attention to visual information.
e.g., <u>wouldn't</u> (substitution)
  couldn't (text)

Oral Reading Rate: (Optional) Use the formula below to determine the student's exact oral reading rate. Convert the student's reading time to all seconds.

2 210 (words) ÷ __89__ total seconds = __2.36__ WPS × 60 = __141__ WPM

DRA Continuum

• Use the information from the Student Reading Survey and the Student Booklet to circle the descriptors that best describe the student's responses for Reading Engagement and Comprehension.
• Add the circled numbers to obtain a total score for each section.
• Record the total scores at the top of page 1. Record the Comprehension score at the top of page 5 after the colon.
Note: If the Comprehension score is less than 14, administer *DRA2* with a lower level text.

235

DRA2 Online Management System

If you are a *DRA2 Online* customer, you would enter the student's oral reading time. The Words-Per-Minute fluency rate will be automatically calculated for you.

STEP 2 Complete the Continuum page.

Use the information recorded and/or checked on the Teacher Observation Guide. Circle the number of the descriptor that best describes the reader's behaviors and responses in each row on the Continuum.

DRA2 CONTINUUM — LEVEL 8 — EARLY READER

	EMERGING	DEVELOPING	INDEPENDENT	ADVANCED
Reading Engagement				
Book Selection	1 Selects new texts from identified leveled sets with teacher support; uncertain about a favorite book	2 Selects new texts from identified leveled sets with moderate support; tells about favorite book in general terms	③ Selects new texts from identified leveled sets most of the time; identifies favorite book by title and tells about a particular event	4 Selects a variety of new texts that are "just right"; identifies favorite book by title and gives an overview of the book
Sustained Reading	1 Sustains independent reading for a short period of time with much encouragement	② Sustains independent reading with moderate encouragement	3 Sustains independent reading for at least 5 minutes at a time	4 Sustains independent reading for an extended period of time
Score	2 3	4 ⑤	6 7	8
Oral Reading Fluency				
Phrasing	1 Reads word-by-word	② Reads word-by-word with some short phrases	3 Reads in short phrases most of the time	4 Reads in longer phrases at times
Monitoring/Self-Corrections	1 Self-corrects no miscues	2 Self-corrects at least 1 miscue and neglects to self-correct other miscues	③ Self-corrects 2 or more miscues or only makes 1 uncorrected miscue	4 Self-corrects miscues quickly or reads accurately
Problem-Solving Unknown Words	1 Stops at difficulty, relying on support to problem-solve unknown words; 3 or more words told by the teacher	2 At difficulty, initiates problem-solving of a few unknown words; 1 or 2 words told by the teacher	3 At difficulty, uses 1 or 2 cues to problem-solve unknown words	④ At difficulty, uses multiple cues to problem-solve unknown words
Accuracy	1 92% or less	2 93%	3 94%–97%	④ 98%–100%
Score	4 5 6	7 8 9 10	11 12 ⑬ 14	15 16
Comprehension				
Previewing	1 Comments briefly about each event or action only when prompted or is uncertain	2 Identifies and comments briefly about each event or action with some prompting	④ Identifies and connects at least 3 key events without prompting; some relevant vocabulary	4 Identifies and connects at least 4 key events without prompting; relevant vocabulary
Retelling: Sequence of Events	1 Includes only 1 or 2 events or details (limited retelling)	2 Includes at least 3 events, generally in random order (partial retelling)	③ Includes most of the important events from the beginning, middle, and end, generally in sequence	4 Includes all important events from the beginning, middle, and end in sequence
Retelling: Characters and Details	1 Refers to characters using general pronouns; may include incorrect information	2 Refers to characters using appropriate pronouns; includes at least 1 detail; may include some misinterpretation	3 Refers to most characters by name and includes some important details	④ Refers to all characters by name and includes most of the important details
	2 Uses some language/vocabulary from the text; some understanding of key words/concepts	3 Uses language/vocabulary from the text; basic understanding of most key words/concepts	④ Uses important language/vocabulary from the text; good understanding of key words/concepts	
	② Retells with 3 or 4 questions or prompts	3 Retells with 1 or 2 questions or prompts	4 Retells with no questions or prompts	
	2 Gives a limited response and/or a general reason for opinion	③ Gives a specific story event/action and a relevant reason for response (e.g., personal connection)	4 Gives a response and reason that reflects higher-level thinking (e.g., synthesis/inference)	
	2 Makes a connection that reflects a limited understanding of the story	③ Makes a literal connection that reflects a basic understanding of the story	4 Makes a thoughtful connection that reflects a deeper understanding of the story	
	14 15 16 17 18	19 20 21 ㉒ 23 24 25	26 27 28	

...ies on the DRA2 Focus for Instruction on the next page.

49

DRA2 CONTINUUM — LEVEL 38 — EXTENDING READER

	INTERVENTION	INSTRUCTIONAL	INDEPENDENT	ADVANCED
Reading Engagement				
Wide Reading	1 Title(s) below grade level; limited reading experiences and book knowledge	2 Titles slightly below grade level; rather limited reading experiences	③ Titles within 2 genres or multiple books within a genre; generally on-grade-level texts	4 Titles across 3 or more genres; many on- and above-grade-level texts
Self-Assessment/Goal Setting	1 No strengths and/or goals	2 General strength(s) and goal(s) related to the reading process	③ 2 specific strengths and 2 specific goals related to the reading process	4 3 specific strengths and 3 specific goals that reflect a higher level of thinking
Score	2 3	4 5	⑥ 7	8
Oral Reading Fluency				
Expression	1 Little expression; monotone	2 Some expression that conveys meaning	③ Expression emphasizing key phrases and words at times	4 Expression emphasizing key phrases and words most of the time
Phrasing	1 Mostly word-by-word	2 Short phrases most of the time; inappropriate pauses	3 Longer phrases most of the time; heeds most punctuation	④ Consistently longer, meaningful phrases; heeds all punctuation
Rate	1 69 WPM or less	2 70–89 WPM	3 90–125 WPM	④ 126 WPM or more
Accuracy	1 94% or less	2 95%	3 96%–98%	④ 99%–100%
Score	4 5 6	7 8 9 10	11 12 13 14	⑮ 16
Comprehension				
Prediction	① Unrelated question(s) or no response	2 At least 1 reasonable question related to the text	3 At least 2 reasonable questions that go beyond page(s) read aloud	4 3 thoughtful questions that go beyond page(s) read aloud
Nonfiction Text Features	1 Limited information accessed from text features or no response	2 Partial information accessed from text features	3 Accurate information accessed from text features	④ Detailed information accessed from text features
Scaffolded Summary	1 1–2 ideas/facts in own language and/or copied text; may include incorrect information	2 Partial summary; generally in own language; some important ideas/facts; may include misinterpretations	③ Summary in own language; includes important ideas and few supporting facts from each section	4 Summary in own language; includes the most important ideas and supporting facts from each section
Scaffolded Summary: Vocabulary	1 General terms or labels; limited understanding of key words/concepts	2 Some language/vocabulary from the text; some understanding of key words/concepts	③ Most language/vocabulary from the text; basic understanding of most key words/concepts	4 All important language/vocabulary from the text; good understanding of key words/concepts
Literal Comprehension	1 Incorrect response or no response	2 Partial response; may include misinterpretation	3 Accurate response	④ Accurate response with specific details
Interpretation	1 Little or no understanding of important text implications	2 Some understanding of important text implications; no supporting details	③ Understands important text implications; may include supporting details	4 Insightful understanding of important text implications with supporting details or rationale
Reflection	1 Insignificant message; no reason for opinion or no response	2 Less significant message and/or a general reason for opinion	3 Significant message and a relevant reason for opinion	④ Significant message and reason for opinion that reflects higher-level thinking
Score	7 8 9 10 11 12 13	14 15 16 17 18	19 20 21 ㉒ 23 24 25	26 27 28

Choose three to five teaching/learning activities on the DRA2 Focus for Instruction on the next page.

236

Reading Engagement

Levels A–24

③ Use your daily classroom observations and the student's responses to the Reading Engagement questions/prompts to select descriptors that best describe his or her level of Reading Engagement.

Levels 28–40

④ Use the student's responses on the Student Reading Survey to select descriptors that best describe his or her level of Reading Engagement.

Comprehension

Directions for scoring students' responses to comprehension questions or prompts, as well as examples of these responses, are included in the Handbook, starting on page 88.

Levels 4–24

5 Use information from the student's oral retelling noted on the Story Overview to select the descriptors on the Continuum that best reflect his or her performance.

Student Booklet   *Mae Jemison*

LITERAL COMPREHENSION

List 3 things that Mae learned to do in the astro

Mae learned...

6
1. How to use the space
2. What it was like in space.
3. What the suit did.

INTERPRETATION

Why do you think Mae wanted to be an astron

was instrid in space science.

REFLECTION

What do you think is the most important thing that you learned from this book?

That you can be anything that you want to be when you grow up.

Tell why you think it is important. Because back then not all women could be anything they wanted.

Reread what you have written to make sure your answers are the way you want them before you hand in your booklet.

240

Name/Date   Teacher/Grade   Level 8, Page 5

DRA2 CONTINUUM	LEVEL 8		EARLY READER
	EMERGING	DEVELOPING	INDEPENDENT	ADVANCED

Reading Engagement

	EMERGING	DEVELOPING	INDEPENDENT	ADVANCED
Book Selection	1 Selects new texts from identified leveled sets with teacher support; uncertain about a favorite book	2 Selects new texts from identified leveled sets with moderate support; tells about favorite book in general terms	③ Selects new texts from identified leveled sets most of the time; identifies favorite book by title and tells about a particular event	4 Selects a variety of new texts that are "just right"; identifies favorite book by title and gives an overview of the book
Sustained Reading	1 Sustains independent reading for a short period of time with much encouragement	② Sustains independent reading with moderate encouragement	3 Sustains independent reading for at least 5 minutes at a time	4 Sustains independent reading for an extended period of time
Score	2 3	4 ⑤	6 7	8

Oral Reading Fluency

	EMERGING	DEVELOPING	INDEPENDENT	ADVANCED
Phrasing	1 Reads word-by-word	② Reads word-by-word with some short phrases	3 Reads in short phrases most of the time	4 Reads in longer phrases at times
Monitoring/Self-Corrections	1 Self-corrects no miscues	2 Self-corrects at least 1 miscue and neglects to self-correct other miscues	③ Self-corrects 2 or more miscues or only makes 1 uncorrected miscue	4 Self-corrects miscues quickly or reads accurately
Problem-Solving Unknown Words	1 Stops at difficulty, relying on support to problem-solve unknown words; 3 or more words told by the teacher	2 At difficulty, initiates problem-solving of a few unknown words; 1 or 2 words told by the teacher	3 At difficulty, uses 1 or 2 cues to problem-solve unknown words	④ At difficulty, uses multiple cues to problem-solve unknown words
Accuracy	1 92% or less	2 93%	3 94%–97%	④ 98%–100%
Score	4 5 6	7 8 9 10	11 12 ⑬ 14	15 16

Comprehension

	EMERGING	DEVELOPING	INDEPENDENT	ADVANCED
Previewing	1 Comments briefly about each event or action only when prompted or is uncertain	2 Identifies and comments briefly about each event or action with some prompting	③ Identifies and connects at least 3 key events without prompting; some relevant vocabulary	4 Identifies and connects at least 4 key events without prompting; relevant vocabulary
Retelling: Sequence of Events	1 Includes only 1 or 2 events or details (limited retelling)	2 Includes at least 3 events, generally in random order (partial retelling)	③ Includes most of the important events from the beginning, middle, and end, generally in sequence	4 Includes all important events from the beginning, middle, and end in sequence
Retelling: Characters and Details	1 Refers to characters using general pronouns; may include incorrect information	2 Refers to characters using appropriate pronouns; includes at least 1 detail; may include some misinterpretation	3 Refers to most characters by name and includes some important details	④ Refers to all characters by name and includes most of the important details
Retelling: Vocabulary	1 Uses general terms or labels; limited understanding of key words/concepts	2 Uses some language/vocabulary from the text; some understanding of key words/concepts	3 Uses language/vocabulary from the text; basic understanding of most key words/concepts	④ Uses important language/vocabulary from the text; good understanding of key words/concepts
Retelling: Teacher Support	1 Retells with 5 or more questions or prompts	② Retells with 3 or 4 questions or prompts	3 Retells with 1 or 2 questions or prompts	4 Retells with no questions or prompts
Reflection	1 Gives an unrelated response, no reason for opinion, or no response	2 Gives a limited response and/or a general reason for opinion	③ Gives a specific story event/action and a relevant reason for response (e.g., personal connection)	4 Gives a response and reason that reflects higher-level thinking (e.g., synthesis/inference)
Making Connections	1 Makes an unrelated connection, relates an event in the story, or gives no response	2 Makes a connection that reflects a limited understanding of the story	③ Makes a literal connection that reflects a basic understanding of the story	4 Makes a thoughtful connection that reflects a deeper understanding of the story
Score	7 8 9 10 11 12 13	14 15 16 17 18	19 20 21 ㉒ 23 24 25	26 27 28

Choose three to five teaching/learning activities on the *DRA2* Focus for Instruction on the next page.

49

Levels 28–40

6 Use information from the Student Booklet and the examples in the Handbook of this guide to select the descriptors on the Continuum that best reflect the student's performance.

Additional guidelines for interpreting and scoring student responses can be found on Handbook pages 70–119 in the back of this Teacher Guide.

Step 2 continued...

7 Add the circled numbers to obtain a total score for each section.

8 Record the Comprehension score at the top of the Continuum page using the level-colon format.

Mae Jemison 38

8 Level 38, Page 5

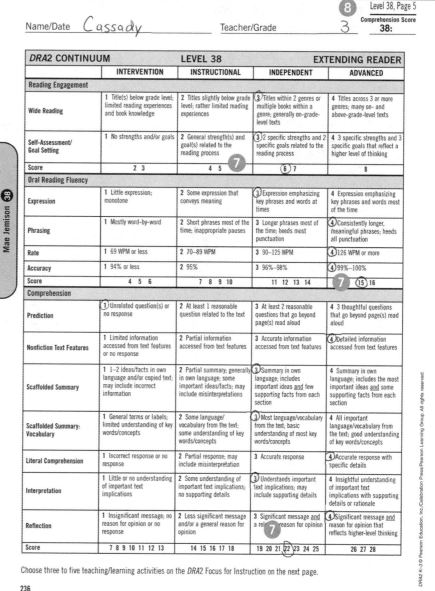

Name/Date Cassady Teacher/Grade 3 Comprehension Score 38:

*DRA*2 CONTINUUM	LEVEL 38			EXTENDING READER
	INTERVENTION	INSTRUCTIONAL	INDEPENDENT	ADVANCED
Reading Engagement				
Wide Reading	1 Title(s) below grade level; limited reading experiences and book knowledge	2 Titles slightly below grade level; rather limited reading experiences	(3) Titles within 2 genres or multiple books within a genre; generally on-grade-level texts	4 Titles across 3 or more genres; many on- and above-grade-level texts
Self-Assessment/ Goal Setting	1 No strengths and/or goals	2 General strength(s) and goal(s) related to the reading process	(3) 2 specific strengths and 2 specific goals related to the reading process	4 3 specific strengths and 3 specific goals that reflect a higher level of thinking
Score	2 3	4 5 7	(6) 7	8
Oral Reading Fluency				
Expression	1 Little expression; monotone	2 Some expression that conveys meaning	(3) Expression emphasizing key phrases and words at times	4 Expression emphasizing key phrases and words most of the time
Phrasing	1 Mostly word-by-word	2 Short phrases most of the time; inappropriate pauses	3 Longer phrases most of the time; heeds most punctuation	(4) Consistently longer, meaningful phrases; heeds all punctuation
Rate	1 69 WPM or less	2 70–89 WPM	3 90–125 WPM	(4) 126 WPM or more
Accuracy	1 94% or less	2 95%	3 96%–98%	(4) 99%–100%
Score	4 5 6	7 8 9 10	11 12 13 14	7 (15) 16
Comprehension				
Prediction	(1) Unrelated question(s) or no response	2 At least 1 reasonable question related to the text	3 At least 2 reasonable questions that go beyond page(s) read aloud	4 3 thoughtful questions that go beyond page(s) read aloud
Nonfiction Text Features	1 Limited information accessed from text features or no response	2 Partial information accessed from text features	3 Accurate information accessed from text features	(4) Detailed information accessed from text features
Scaffolded Summary	1 1–2 ideas/facts in own language and/or copied text; may include incorrect information	2 Partial summary; generally in own language; some important ideas/facts; may include misinterpretations	(3) Summary in own language; includes important ideas <u>and</u> few supporting facts from each section	4 Summary in own language; includes the most important ideas <u>and</u> some supporting facts from each section
Scaffolded Summary: Vocabulary	1 General terms or labels; limited understanding of key words/concepts	2 Some language/ vocabulary from the text; some understanding of key words/concepts	(3) Most language/vocabulary from the text; basic understanding of most key words/concepts	4 All important language/vocabulary from the text; good understanding of key words/concepts
Literal Comprehension	1 Incorrect response or no response	2 Partial response; may include misinterpretation	3 Accurate response	(4) Accurate response with specific details
Interpretation	1 Little or no understanding of important text implications	2 Some understanding of important text implications; no supporting details	(3) Understands important text implications; may include supporting details	4 Insightful understanding of important text implications with supporting details or rationale
Reflection	1 Insignificant message; no reason for opinion or no response	2 Less significant message and/or a general reason for opinion	3 Significant message <u>and</u> a rel[7] reason for opinion	(4) Significant message <u>and</u> reason for opinion that reflects higher-level thinking
Score	7 8 9 10 11 12 13	14 15 16 17 18	19 20 21 (22) 23 24 25	26 27 28

Choose three to five teaching/learning activities on the *DRA*2 Focus for Instruction on the next page.

236

Levels 4–24

For an Independent level the student's total Oral Reading Fluency score and total Comprehension score must be at least within the Independent range on the Continuum. If the student's scores are below Independent, reassess with a lower-level text at another time.*

Levels 28–40

For an Independent level the student's total Oral Reading Fluency score and total Comprehension score must be at least within the Independent range on the Continuum.

If a student's Comprehension score is less than 19 for Levels 4–24, less than 14 for Levels 28–38, or less than 12 for Level 40 select a lower-level assessment text and conduct a second *DRA*2 conference on another day. (Omit the Reading Engagement questions this time.)*

Students reading text Levels 28–40 are not reassessed using a lower *DRA*2 level text if their total comprehension score falls within the Instructional range on the Continuum. Without instruction it is highly improbable that they will perform any better when asked to write similar responses with a slightly lower-level text.

It is important to teach Extending readers how to respond in writing to demonstrate their comprehension. Providing opportunities to respond in writing scaffolds their ability to think more deeply about a text and prepares them for proficiency tests at the district and state levels.

***Note:** If the student has previously read and scored within an Independent range in Oral Reading Fluency and Comprehension on the lower-level text, it is not necessary to administer another assessment.

STEP 3 Complete the DRA2 Focus for Instruction page.

Levels 2–12

9 Use the features on the Continuum that you identified as Emerging and Developing as a guide to help you select 3 to 5 learning/teaching activities on the Focus for Instruction.

Teacher Observation Guide   *Duke*   Level 8, Page 6

DRA2 FOCUS FOR INSTRUCTION FOR EARLY READERS

READING ENGAGEMENT

Book Selection
- ☐ Provide guided opportunities to select familiar stories for rereading
- ☐ Model and support how to select "just right" new texts for independent reading
- ☐ Model and discuss why readers have favorite books and authors

Sustained Reading
- ☑ Model and support the use of sustained reading time
- ☑ Create structures and routines to support buddy reading
- ☐ Create structures and routines to support reading at home

ORAL READING FLUENCY

Phrasing
- ☐ Encourage student to read in phrases during shared reading
- ☐ Show how words are grouped into phrases in big books and poetry charts
- ☑ Support rereading familiar texts to build fluency

Monitoring/Self-Corrections
- ☐ Support one-to-one matching as a means to self-monitor
- ☐ Model and teach how to use known words as a means to self-monitor
- ☐ Model and support confirming and discounting word choice using meaning, language, and visual information
- ☐ Demonstrate and teach how to read for meaning, self-correcting when a word doesn't make sense or sound right
- ☐ Model and teach how to monitor visual information, self-correcting when a word doesn't look right

Problem-Solving Unknown Words
- ☐ Model and support using beginning letter(s)/sound(s), sentence and/or story structure, as well as meaning (illustrations and background knowledge) to problem-solve unknown words
- ☐ Model and support how to take words apart (onset and rime) to problem-solve unknown words

COMPREHENSION

Previewing
- ☐ Support creating a story from the illustrations
- ☐ Model and support previewing a book before reading, during read-aloud and shared reading experiences

Retelling
- ☑ Model the retelling of familiar stories
- ☐ Model and teach the elements in a good retelling
- ☐ Demonstrate how to create and use story maps to aid retelling
- ☐ Support retelling a story in sequence
- ☐ Encourage student to use characters' names when retelling a story
- ☐ Model and support using key language/vocabulary from the text in a retelling

Response: Reflection
- ☐ Support and reinforce student's response to books during read-aloud, and shared and guided reading experiences
- ☐ Help student identify favorite part of books
- ☐ Provide opportunities to select a favorite book, toy, TV show, etc., and tell why it is a favorite
- ☐ Demonstrate how to give reason(s) for one's opinion

Response: Making Connections
- ☐ Model and teach how to make text-to-self connections
- ☐ Model and support how to make text-to-text connections

OTHER

_____
_____
_____
_____
_____
_____

Duke 8

50

DRA2 Online Management System

If you are a *DRA2 Online* customer, you would enter information into the computer for the descriptor numbers you circled on a student's assessment. The system will then create for you a complete Continuum report along with computed scores for that student. The highlighted sections on the Continuum report represent the items you circled. The system will then provide you with suggested marked items on the Focus for Instruction.

If you are using the *DRA Online Writer*, your complete assessment will automatically be uploaded into the computer and a Continuum report will be generated without your having to enter data.

Assessment Guidelines

STEP 3 continued...

Levels 14–40

10 Use the features on the Continuum that you identified as Intervention and Instructional as a guide to help you select 3 to 5 learning/teaching activities on the Focus for Instruction.

Teacher Observation Guide **Mae Jemison** Level 38, Page 6

DRA2 FOCUS FOR INSTRUCTION FOR EXTENDING READERS

READING ENGAGEMENT

Wide Reading
- ☐ Teach student strategies to select appropriately leveled texts for independent reading
- ☒ Introduce student to reading materials from a variety of genres
- ☐ Teach strategies to build reading stamina
- ☐ Create structures and/or routines to support reading at home
- ☐ Develop clear expectations for amount of independent reading
- ☐ Teach student how to use a reading log to monitor book selection and set reading goals
- ☐ Model/teach how to read for different purposes

Self-Assessment/Goal Setting
- ☐ Model and discuss strategies good readers use
- ☐ Help student identify 1–2 reading goals and a plan of action to improve reading
- ☐ Support revision of ongoing reading goals

ORAL READING FLUENCY

Expression and Phrasing
- ☐ Model and support reading in longer, meaningful phrases with appropriate expression
- ☐ Have student practice appropriate expression with familiar texts
- ☐ Teach student to recognize and emphasize key phrases and words in nonfiction texts
- ☐ Teach student to heed punctuation

Rate
- ☐ Provide materials and time for repeated reading to increase reading rate
- ☐ Teach student to read lower level and/or familiar texts at an appropriate rate

Accuracy: Word Analysis
- ☐ Support and reinforce self-corrections of miscues
- ☐ Model and support how to take words apart (e.g., onset and rime, syllables) to problem-solve unknown words in nonfiction texts
- ☐ Teach how to use word chunks and analogies to problem-solve unknown words

COMPREHENSION

10 **Prediction**
- ☒ Provide opportunities for student to make predictions based on title, table of contents, and headings
- ☐ Model and support using background information to make meaningful predictions
- ☐ Model and teach student how to pose questions as a basis for predictions

Nonfiction Text Features
- ☐ Model and support how to read and interpret charts, graphs, maps, tables, etc.
- ☐ Model and teach how to use table of contents, headings, glossary, etc.

Summary
- ☐ Share and identify characteristics of good summaries
- ☐ Model and co-construct written summaries of texts read aloud
- ☐ Model and support how to distinguish between more important and less important ideas and facts
- ☐ Model and support how to write a summary in one's own words
- ☐ Model and support how to use examples from the text
- ☐ Teach student how to use headings to organize a summary of an informational/nonfiction text

Literal Comprehension
- ☐ Show student how to use key words to identify specific information from the text
- ☐ Provide opportunities for student to answer and construct literal questions
- ☐ Teach student how to use graphic organizers to keep track of key ideas and facts

Interpretation
- ☐ Teach and share examples of inferences
- ☐ Provide opportunities for student to support inferences with information or examples from the text
- ☐ Give student opportunities to respond to inference questions orally and in writing
- ☐ Model and support how to interpret nonfiction text features (e.g., how to read a chart or diagram)

Reflection
- ☐ Help student identify important information and key vocabulary
- ☐ Demonstrate how to support opinion with details from the text

237

Mae Jemison **38**

DRA2 Online Management System

After you submit your assessment online, the system will generate an Assessment Summary Report for each student.

Determining Proficiency

Students learn to read and develop as readers at different rates. Using *DRA2* periodically enables you to monitor changes over time in students' reading performances and confirms ongoing observations and impressions of student reading achievement.

Some students may need additional literacy instruction and support in learning how to read. The school or school district will need to establish benchmarks to identify those students who are performing below proficiency. The following chart gives suggested benchmarks for the fall and spring of each grade level.

*Note: These benchmark levels would need to be adjusted if the *DRA2* is given at other times during the school year.

Grade	Time of Year	*DRA2* Benchmark Level*
Kindergarten	January May/June	1 3
First Grade	September May/June	3–6 16–18
Second Grade	September May/June	16–20 28
Third Grade	September May/June	28–34 38

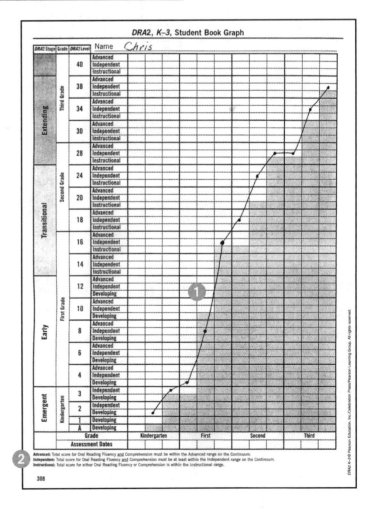

1 Plot the student's progress on the Student Book Graph by filling in or marking the appropriate section for the text level assessed.

2 Use the directions to determine if the text is on the student's Independent or Instructional level.

60

Grouping for Instruction

Focus for Instruction: Class Profile

The Focus for Instruction: Class Profile form enables teachers to decide how to group students for instruction based on specific needs. *DRA2, K–3*, offers a form for each reading stage: Emergent, Early, Transitional, and Extending.

STEP 1 Fill out the form to create a class list.

Write each student's first name and initial of last name if needed and then check the areas needing instruction in Reading Engagement, Oral Reading Fluency, and/or Comprehension.

STEP 2 Determine the most effective ways to group students.

The organization of groups will depend on the number of students needing the same type of instruction or reading at similar levels.

Note that text level is just one factor to consider when grouping students for instruction. Students reading at the same level may need help with different areas of instruction. For example, some may need help with comprehension strategies while others may need help with phrasing and expression or word analysis skills and strategies.

DRA2 Online Management System

DRA2 Online users do not need to use the Class Profile Form, as the system will generate instructional groupings based on students' needs. All you need to do is select the categories in the Focus for Instruction in which you would like to group students, or select all of the categories. You would then select the group or groups for which you want a Focus for Instruction report. You can, at any time, change the groups you have created.

DRA2, K–3, Focus for Instruction: Class Profile for Transitional Readers

Levels 14–24

Grade Level: 2nd   Date: Fall 2005

Names	Text Level	Reading Engagement		Oral Reading Fluency			Comprehension					
		Book Selection	Sustained Reading	Expression and Phrasing	Rate	Accuracy: Word Analysis	Previewing/Prediction	Retelling	Using Nonfiction Text Features	Reflection	Making Connections	Interpretation
1. Chris	14			✓	✓		✓	✓			✓	
2. Fred	24			✓		✓	✓			✓		✓
3. Sarah	16F				✓				✓	✓	✓	✓
4. Amy	18		✓	✓	✓			✓				✓
5. John	19			✓		✓	✓	✓				
6. Yakim	20			✓								
7. Cho	24									✓		✓
8. Mark	18	✓				✓		✓			✓	
9. Brandon	18		✓				✓			✓	✓	✓
10. Maggie	14	✓			✓			✓				✓
11. Joseph	24						✓			✓		✓
12. Kim	16F	✓			✓			✓		✓	✓	
13. Adam	16NF	✓				✓		✓	✓			✓
14.												
15.												
16.												
17.												
18.												
19.												
20.												
21.												
22.												
23.												
24.												
25.												

Record students' names and check the areas selected as a focus for instruction. For students reading at Level 16, use **F** to indicate fiction and **NF** to indicate nonfiction next to the text level (e.g., 16F or 16NF).

311

Conducting Further Assessments

Further assessments are especially important for students who are performing below established benchmarks. The goal is to find a text level at which students can read independently with adequate comprehension and fluency. Even if students qualify for other support services, classroom teachers need to know what text levels students are able to read and understand independently. Then they can plan effectively and implement appropriate teaching/learning activities within the classroom.

STEP 1 Identify the emerging and struggling readers who are performing below proficiency.

Use the Benchmark Assessment Book levels selected by the school or district to identify those students who are performing below proficiency. You may keep track of them on the Class Reporting Form.

STEP 2 Conduct one or more of the following assessments.

You can use one or more of the following assessments to obtain further information about what emerging or struggling readers control and what is most important for them to learn next.

Level A or 1 Assessment

If a student is unable to read Level A or 1, ask the student to read

- his or her first name printed on an index card
- names of other family members printed on index cards
- environmental print, such as food containers, cereal boxes, and so on

Oral Reading Accuracy

If a student's Oral Reading Accuracy falls in the Emerging or Developing (Levels A–12) or Intervention or Instructional (Levels 14–28) range of performance due to insufficient word analysis skills and strategies, conduct the *DRA Word Analysis*. You can then observe how these readers attend to and work with the various components of spoken and written words.

DRA Word Analysis is divided into five strands: (1) phonological awareness, (2) metalanguage (language used to talk about printed language concepts), (3) letter/word recognition, (4) phonics, and (5) structural analysis and syllabication. The tasks, as much as possible, reflect what developing readers need to know and do in order to successfully problem-solve unknown or less familiar words as they read connected, meaningful texts.

Documenting Change Over Time

The Continuum within the Teacher Observation Guide and the *DRA2, K–3,* Student Assessment Folder can be used to document students' achievement. These forms reflect the individual student's present level of performance, as well as his or her progress over time. Each year, the Teacher Observation Guides (A–40), as well as Extending readers' (Levels 28–40) Student Reading Surveys and Student Booklets are stored inside the folder.

1 Record the date, the student's *DRA2* text level, as well as the performance level on the front of the folder.

2 Place the student's Teacher Observation Guide, as well as the Student Reading Survey and Student Booklet for Extending readers, in the pockets inside the folder. All assessment forms for nonfiction are stored in the left-side pocket and fiction in the right-side pocket.

3 Record the date, Benchmark Assessment Book title, *DRA2* Independent level, percent of accuracy, total Reading Engagement, Oral Reading Fluency, and Comprehension score on the appropriate line.

Note: For students reading text levels 28–40, place an asterisk after the text level if the student's Comprehension score is below the Independent range.

4 On the back, plot the assessment text level on the Student Book Graph. The shaded area on the graph represents below-grade-level performance.

These forms are also available in the Blackline Masters book and on the Blackline Masters CD.

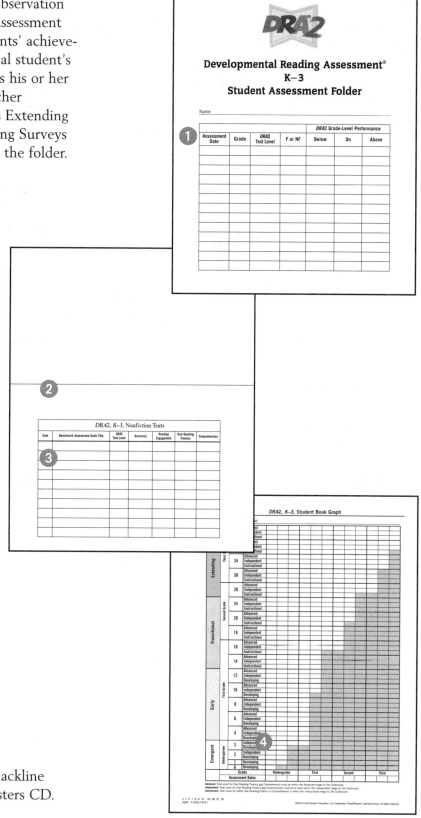

Guidelines for Identifying an Instructional-Level Text

When a student's total score for Oral Reading Fluency or Comprehension falls within the Instructional range on the *DRA2* Continuum, the level of the text read by the student is identified as an Instructional level.

If you are directed to find an instructional level for each student, follow these guidelines.

1. **Oral Reading Fluency**
   - Stop the assessment after the record of oral reading if the student's score for words-per-minute or accuracy falls within the Intervention range on the charts. Reassess with a lower-level text.*
   - Continue the assessment even if the student's score for words-per-minute or accuracy falls within or above the Independent range on the charts.

2. **Comprehension**
   - Reassess with a lower-level text at another time if the student's total Comprehension score falls within the Intervention range on the Continuum.*
   - Reassess with the next level text at another time if the student scored within an Independent range in Oral Reading Fluency and Comprehension on the Continuum.

   *Note: If the student has previously read and scored within an Independent range in Oral Reading Fluency and Comprehension on the preceding text level, it is not necessary to administer another assessment.

3. *DRA2* **Focus for Instruction**
   - Consider the items that fell within the Instructional or Intervention level on the Continuum and identify the ones that will have the greatest impact on student learning.
   - Select three to five teaching/learning activities on the *DRA2* Focus for Instruction that will address those skills/strategies.

4. **Reporting Forms**
   - On the Student Book Graph, plot the student's current Instructional level by filling in or marking the Instructional section for the text level assessed.
   - Place an asterisk after any *DRA2* text title or level that is identified as an Instructional level on the front or inside the Student Assessment Folder.
   - Indicate at the bottom of the Class Reporting Form that the *DRA2* level text listed for each student is an Instructional level.

Sharing the Results

Use the Class Reporting Form to share the assessment results with school and/or district administrators.

You may use this form to record students' *DRA2* text levels and Continuum scores for school or district administrators. This information can be used to identify students who remain at risk in their development as readers and are in need of further assessments and/or other support services.

For ease in tracking changes in student reading behaviors over the school year, make several copies of this reporting form (located in the Blackline Masters book and CD). Determine how many times you will administer the assessment during the year (usually two or three), and then write students' names on alternating lines or every third line. This approach allows new assessment data to be entered right under the student's name.

- If you plan to administer the assessment twice a year, skipping a line between student names will permit you to enter the end-of-year data on the blank line directly under the fall data.
- If you plan to administer the assessment three times a year, skip two lines between students' names to provide space for data to be recorded for the two remaining assessment periods.
- For students reading text Levels 28–40, place as asterisk after the text level if the student's Comprehension score is below the Independent range.
- Enter the scores for each category on the chart. For Levels A–3 enter the Printed Language Concepts score in the last column. For Levels 4–40 enter the Comprehension score in the last column.

DRA2, K–3, Class Reporting Form

Teacher __Thos__   School __Barrington__   Grade __2nd__   Date __2005__

Names	Text Level (F/NF)	Reading Engagement Score	Oral Reading Fluency Score	Printed Language Concepts/ Comprehension Score
Chris	14F	5	11	19
Fred	24F	7	13	22
Sarah	16 NF	7	12	19
Amy	18F	6	12	19
John	18F	7	14	21
Yakim	20F	7	11	20
Cho	28NF*	8	13	16
Nadia	30 F*	7	15	17
Ashee	10 F	6	11	20
Mark	18F	6	12	23
Brandon	18F	6	13	20
Maggie	14 F	6	12	17

Highlight the names of the students who are reading below the grade-level benchmark. For students reading Levels 28–40, place an asterisk after the text level if the Comprehension Score is below Independent.

DRA2 K–3 © Pearson Education, Inc./Celebration Press/Pearson Learning Group. All rights reserved.

313

Share assessment results and changes over time in student reading performance with families at conferences and in progress reports.

The results of *DRA2, K–3,* also can be shared with parents. The information on the Continuum and the Student Assessment Folder helps parents to understand and appreciate their child's reading progress, as well as strengths and needs in specific areas (Reading Engagement, Oral Reading Fluency, and Comprehension). After seeing the specific components on the Continuum, parents also have a better understanding of what you are trying to accomplish. Many of the statements on the Continuum may be used on students' progress reports as well.

Discussing the Student Book Graph on the back of the Student Assessment Folder enables parents to see their child's present reading level. The graph also shows the progress the student has made over time.

Share assessment results with students when they are able to understand them and are beginning to select personal reading goals.

Sharing their Continuums with Extending readers (text Levels 28–38) helps these students know what is expected and provides them with the language to discuss and evaluate their own performance as readers. The Continuum also enables students to identify what they do well and what they need to work on to become better readers. In addition, it helps them to select appropriate reading goals in Reading Engagement, Oral Reading Fluency, and/or Comprehension. When Extending readers are given the opportunity to set personal reading goals, it gives them a sense of control and creates a more positive attitude toward learning and reading.

DRA2 Online Management System

DRA2 Online provides more than one type of report that keeps track of each student's progress over time. These reports also make it easy to share assessment information with families and other colleagues.

- You can access the assessment history for a student, which is helpful in selecting Focus for Instruction items based on previous assessments.
- The Reading Stage Performance Report shows your class's progress through reading stages.
- The Reading Level Performance Chart shows your class's performance and progress compared to benchmarked levels.
- Word Analysis Cumulative Report shows a student's progress on *DRA Word Analysis* over time.
- Also available as reports are all of the additional forms available in the Blackline Masters book. These include the Class Profile: Focus for Instruction, the Class Reporting Form, and the Student Book Graph. These reports will help you keep track of the progress individual students, as well as your class, make over multiple assessments.

Developmental Reading Assessment®

K–3

Handbook

Analyzing Student Performance: Descriptions and Examples

In *DRA2, K–3*, there are consistent and clear criteria on the Continuums for scoring student responses. Students can meet these criteria by using a variety of responses. Please note that there is more than one correct answer for each response. It is the amount of clarity, appropriateness of content, and insight demonstrated in the response that generally determines the level of performance.

To ensure reliable scoring, it is essential that you become familiar with the criteria used for establishing performance levels as well as with the texts that your students will be reading. For this reason, definitions and examples are given in this section of the Teacher Guide to illustrate the types of Independent and Advanced responses for Reading Engagement and Comprehension on the Continuum. You will also find directions for scoring to help you analyze and score students' oral and/or written responses.

On the *DRA2, K–3*, Continuum, a score of
- **4 represents an Advanced performance**
- **3 represents an Independent performance**
- **2 represents either a Developing (Levels A–12) or an Instructional (Levels 14–40) performance**
- **1 represents either an Emerging (Levels A–12) or Intervention (Levels 14–40) performance**

When scoring students' oral and/or written responses, read and consider content only. All structural and/or mechanical errors (grammar, punctuation, and/or spelling) should not be factored into your decision, but they can be noted for instruction.

Authors' Note: Student examples included in this section reflect responses given by students. Spelling has been altered to make the examples easier to read. Generally, no other mechanical or grammatical corrections have been made.

Reading Engagement

Engagement consists of
- **the amount of reading**
- **knowledge of books and authors**
- **the variety of the materials read**
- **personal awareness as a reader**

The Reading Engagement questions help you to become aware of students' preferences and alert you to students who are somewhat passive about reading or have limited literacy experiences. It is important that students not only learn how to read, but that they also spend time reading on a daily basis and find reading enjoyable.

In *DRA2*, Levels A through 24, student oral responses to reading-preference questions and ongoing classroom observations are used to evaluate the student's overall engagement as a reader. The prompts and questions in this section change from the lower to the higher *DRA2* text levels.

Emergent Readers (DRA2 Levels A–3)

For Emergent readers, Reading Engagement includes literacy support, favorite book, and book-handling skills.

Literacy Support refers to the support provided by parents and/or others when they read to or listen to emerging readers.

Being able to tell about a **Favorite Book** indicates that the reader has had the opportunity to hear books read and reread aloud.

Book-Handling Skills demonstrate the reader's ability to control a book while reading and reflect his or her previous experiences with "reading" books independently.

Evaluation of the student's literacy support and ability to identify and tell about a favorite book should be based on his or her responses to prompts given during the assessment. Evaluate the student's skill in holding and turning pages of a book based on your observations.

Examples of Emergent Readers' Reading Engagement Oral Responses		
LITERACY SUPPORT Prompt: *"Who reads with you or to you at home?"*	**Developing Descriptor:** Names at least one person who reads with him or her at home	**Oral-Response Example:** *My mom*
	Independent Descriptor: Names several people who read with him or her at home	**Oral-Response Example:** *Mom, Xavier, Brittany*
FAVORITE BOOK Prompt: *"Tell me about one of your favorite books."*	**Developing Descriptor:** Tells something about a favorite book	**Oral-Response Examples:** 1. *I like the book where the pigeon drives the bus.*
		2. *Care Bears* (Note: Even though this child named a book, the response is scored at the developing level because he/she did not tell about the book.)
	Independent Descriptor: Gives title and shares some specific details about favorite book	**Oral-Response Example:** *Brown Bear* *What Brown Bear and the other animals can see. I can already read it.*
BOOK-HANDLING SKILLS Teacher prompts student to hold or turn a page when needed.	**Emerging Descriptor:** Relies on others to hold and turn pages of a book	
	Developing Descriptor: Holds and/or turns pages of a book when prompted	
	Independent Descriptor: Holds and turns pages of a book independently	

Early and Transitional Readers (DRA2 Levels 4–24)

For Early and Transitional readers, Reading Engagement consists of Book Selection and Sustained Reading.

Book Selection refers to the students' ability to select appropriately leveled books for independent reading, as well as to identify and talk about favorite book(s). Learning how to select appropriately leveled reading materials to fulfill multiple purposes enables students to become more independent in the classroom and have greater control over their choice of reading materials. When students are given opportunities to choose their own texts, they are more likely to read and enjoy reading.

Note: Questions and prompts are included in this section so that you are aware of the student's reading preference(s) and the support the student is receiving at home.

These questions and prompts include:
- **Who reads with you or to you at home?**
- **Would you rather listen to a story or read a story to someone? Why?**
- **Do you like to read alone, with a buddy, or with a group? Why?**
- **How do you choose the books you read?**
- **What kinds of books do you like to read?**
- **Whom do you read with at home?**
- **Tell me about one of your favorite books.**

Sustained Reading refers to the student's ability to read independently for a period of time. The amount of time developing readers are able to read independently increases over time. In this section, evaluate students' ability to select new texts and sustain independent reading based on your ongoing classroom observations.

A student needs to meet all the Independent criteria to be considered independent. If he or she only meets part of the criteria, select the Developing/Instructional descriptor. For example, if a student selects new texts independently most of the time but only gives a book title, or tells about a book in general terms, and/or is uncertain about a favorite book, you would choose the Developing/Instructional descriptor on the Continuum.

The student also needs to meet all Advanced criteria on the Continuum to be considered advanced.

Examples of Early/Transitional Readers' Reading Engagement Oral Responses

BOOK SELECTION	Independent Descriptor:	Oral-Response Examples:
Prompt: *"Tell me about one of your favorite books."*	Selects new texts from identified leveled sets most of the time; identifies favorite book by title and tells about a particular event	1. _Old Hat, New Hat_ In the end he gets his old hat back.
		2. _Henry and Mudge_ When Mudge took the dog test and won
	Advanced Descriptor: Selects a variety of "just right texts"; identifies favorite book by title and gives an overview of the book	Oral-Response Examples: 1. _Cookie's Week_ Cookie climbed up the curtains and fell everywhere. Even though they thought he might rest, I think he will get himself in more trouble.
		2. _But No Elephant_ It's about a guy selling pets. He sells them all except the elephant. Then a girl takes it and it gets stuck in her house.

SUSTAINED READING	Independent Descriptor:
Note: No prompts are given. Your evaluation of a student's ability to sustain independent reading is based on your ongoing classroom observations.	Sustains independent reading for at least _____* minutes at a time *Note the length of time increases over time from 5 minutes to 15 minutes by the end of first grade.
	Advanced Descriptor: Sustains independent reading for an extended period of time

Extending Readers
(DRA2, Levels 28–38)

For Extending readers, evaluate the students' overall engagement as readers based on their written responses to questions and prompts about Wide Reading and Self-Assessment/Goal Setting on the Student Reading Survey.

Wide Reading refers to the type and amount of reading students do on a regular basis. It also gives insight into the students' preferences as readers.

A student needs to meet all Independent criteria in order to be considered independent. If he or she only meets part of the criteria, select the Instructional descriptor. For example, the student lists on-grade-level texts that he or she has finished reading but does not list what he or she is are presently reading at school and/or home.

The student also needs to meet all Advanced criteria on the Continuum to be considered advanced. An advanced student needs to have at least one title from three different genres among six or more book titles listed on the Student Reading Survey.

Examples of Extending Readers' Reading Engagement Written Responses		

WIDE READING
 	
Prompts:
1. What books have you finished reading lately? You may use your record of books read.
 	
2. What are you reading at school and at home now?
	Independent Descriptor:
	Titles within 2 genres or multiple books within a genre; generally on-grade-level texts
		Student Response Examples:
		1. _Sunset of the Sabertooth_
		   Junie B. Jones and Some Monkey Business
		   Mouse Soup
		   Mouse Tales
		
		2. _Handmade Sign Language_
		   Junie B. Jones Loves Handsome Warren

	Advanced Descriptor:
	Titles across 3 or more genres; many on- and above-grade-level texts
		Student Response Examples
		1. _A to Z Mysteries_
		   Helen Keller: Courage in the Dark
		   The Great Houdini
		   Junie B. Jones: Boo and I Mean it!
		
		2. _Series of Unfortunate Events_
		   Junie B. Jones

Engaged readers have a growing understanding about their strengths and needs as readers. They also have goals and some plan of action for themselves as readers. Students' responses to the **Self-Assessment/Goal Setting** questions give you insight into how students perceive themselves as readers, as well as their ability to monitor and reflect upon their reading behaviors.

As in the sections above, a student must meet all the criteria for Independent and/or Advanced on the Continuum to be considered at those levels of performance. If part of the criteria is not met, then select the previous descriptor. For example, if the student identified three strengths (an Advanced response) for self-assessment but identified two goals (an Independent response), you would select the Independent descriptor on the Continuum. If the student identified three strengths (an Advanced response) for self-assessment but identified one goal (an Instructional response), you would select the Instructional descriptor on the Continuum. The student did not meet the criteria for Independent and his or her response indicates a need for instruction in setting goals as a reader.

Examples of Extending Readers' Reading Engagement Written Responses

SELF-ASSESSMENT/ GOAL SETTING		

Prompts:
1. What are 3 things you do well as a reader?
 	
2. What are 3 things you would like to work on to become a better reader?
	Independent Descriptor:
	2 specific strengths and 2 specific goals related to the reading process
		Response Examples:
		1. Strengths:
		  • *think about what I am reading*
		  • *reading with expression*
		2. Goal(s):
		  • *figure out words when there are no pictures*
		  • *read longer chapter books*

		1. Strengths:
		  • *I sound out words*
		  • *I read . and ! and ?*
		2. Goal(s):
		  • *I want to slow down and think about my reading*
		  • *I want to learn to figure out hard words*

	Advanced Descriptor:
	3 specific strengths and 3 specific goals that reflect a higher level of thinking
		Response Examples:
		1. Strengths:
		  • *stopping and thinking about what I am reading*
		  • *making connections*
		  • *read fast*
		2. Goal(s):
		  • *slow down so I don't miss anything*
		  • *try to read more historical fiction*
		  • *make sure I sound like the people talking*

		1. Strengths:
		  • *understanding what I read*
		  • *picking just-right books*
		  • *knowing how to sound out a lot of words*
		2. Goal(s):
		  • *make more predictions in my head*
		  • *read the Magic Tree House books in order*
		  • *understand words I don't know*

Comprehension

The next section of the Handbook provides general directions for scoring students' oral or written responses. Also included are examples of Independent and Advanced student responses to the Comprehension questions and prompts for select Level 4–24 Benchmark Assessment Books and all Level 28-38 Benchmark Assessment Books.

Examples of Developing/Instructional or Emerging/Intervention responses have not been included in this section. It is assumed that if you know what Independent and Advanced responses include, you will recognize a partial or partially correct response. Partial or partially correct responses are scored as Developing/Instructional on the Continuum. Students' responses that are incorrect, very limited, or omitted are scored as Emerging/Intervention on the Continuum.

Constructing meaning before, during, and after reading a text is at the heart of reading. The ability to effectively comprehend, and then retell and/or write a summary that includes important information (e.g., key concepts, facts, and vocabulary in a nonfiction text; important characters, events, and

details in a fiction text) is essential for all successful readers/learners. Students' responses to the prompts and questions given orally and/or in writing in the Student Booklets demonstrate how well they use comprehension skills and strategies to

- **understand the text**
- **think beyond the literal level**
- **support their thoughts with details from the text**

The selected skills and strategies included in the Comprehension section of the *DRA2, K–3*, Continuum change as you move from the lower to the higher text levels.

It is critical that you know the *DRA2* texts that your students are reading. It is impossible to make sound, consistent judgments about students' levels of comprehension if you do not know the stories and nonfiction texts that you are using with students.

DRA2, K–3, Text Levels		4–16	18–24	28–38	40
Comprehension Skills and Strategies	Previewing	Oral			
	Prediction		Oral	Dictated	Written
	Retelling	Oral	Oral		
	Nonfiction Text Features	Oral		Dictated	
	Fiction Text Features			Dictated	
	Summary			Scaffolded/Written	Written
	Making Connections	Oral			
	Reflection	Oral	Oral	Written	Written
	Interpretation		Oral	Written	Written
	Literal Comprehension			Written	Written
	Metacognitive Awareness				Written

Previewing: Description

When students preview a text (Levels 4–16), they use background knowledge, the book title, the introduction given by the teacher, and information from the illustrations to construct a tentative story. In *DRA2, K–3*, students are asked to look at the pictures and tell what is happening in the story.

Note that it is important during the assessment to record in the margin on the Teacher Observation Guide key ideas and vocabulary/names, as well as connecting language that the students included in their preview. These notes will help you make better judgments and support why you selected specific descriptors on the Continuum.

To evaluate a student's preview, note his or her use of connecting language (such as *and, then, now*), as well as the inclusion of key vocabulary, characters, and events depicted in the illustrations. Also consider if the student needed to be prompted during this portion of the assessment.

Select an Advanced performance on the Continuum if the student's preview includes:

- **characters' names given in the introduction**
- **at least four events or actions depicted in the illustrations**
- **key vocabulary given in the introduction or depicted in the illustrations**
- **connecting language/transitional words or phrases (such as *and, then, in the end*) without prompting**

Select an Independent performance if the student's preview includes:

- **characters' names given in the introduction**
- **at least three events or actions depicted in the illustrations**
- **some key vocabulary given in the introduction or depicted in the illustrations**
- **some connecting language/transitional words or phrases (such as *and, then, in the end*) without prompting**

Students must meet all the criteria for the Independent or Advanced performance on the Continuum to be considered at those levels. If part of the criteria is not met, then select either an Emerging/Intervention or Developing/Instructional descriptor.

Select a Developing/Instructional performance if a student

- **comments briefly about each event or action**
- **does not use connecting language**
- **needs to be prompted to tell what else is happening or depicted in the text**

If a student only comments briefly about each event or action when he or she is prompted or is uncertain about what is happening in the illustrations, select an Emerging/Intervention performance.

Prediction: Description

When students predict, they use their knowledge of text structures, background knowledge, book title, cover, and the introductory passage to propose what is likely to occur in the remaining text. The readers' predictions and questions form a purpose for reading and a basis for monitoring their comprehension. In the *DRA2, K–3* (Levels 18–40), after reading a designated passage, students predict what they think will happen in a fiction text. In a nonfiction text, they pose questions they think will be answered based on the title and table of contents.

Note that it is important during the assessment to record as much as possible what students included in their oral predictions in the margins of the Teacher Observation Guide. These notes will not only help you make better judgments but will also document why you selected specific descriptors on the Continuum.

To evaluate a student's predictions, note if the predictions go beyond what was read aloud and if each prediction is different, not just a restatement. Also note the student's use of tentative language (such as *may, might, probably, think*), transitional words and phrases (such as *and, in the end, then*), characters' names, and/or concepts vocabulary included in the introduction or pages read aloud.

Select an Advanced performance on the Continuum if the student makes three or more thoughtful predictions that go beyond what he or she read aloud.

Consider predictions "thoughtful" when it is evident that the student

- based on his or her predictions on the title, ideas/information from the introduction and page(s) read aloud, as well as prior experiences with similar texts
- used tentative language such as *may, might, probably, think*
- included characters' names and/or concepts and key vocabulary without prompting

Select an Independent performance if the student makes at least two reasonable predictions that go beyond what he or she read aloud. Consider predictions "reasonable" when it is evident that the student

- used the ideas/information from the introduction and page(s) read aloud as the primary basis for his or her predictions
- included at least the main characters' names and some concepts and key vocabulary without prompting

The student must meet all the criteria for Independent or Advanced on the Continuum to be considered at one of those levels. If part of the criteria is not met or the student needed prompting, then select either a Developing/Instructional or Emerging/Intervention descriptor.

Select a Developing/Instructional performance when a student makes at least one reasonable prediction based on what he or she has heard in the introduction or read aloud and/or was prompted.

Select an Emerging/Intervention performance if the student makes an unrelated prediction or was uncertain about what might happen in the rest of the text.

Retelling: Description

The oral retelling in the *DRA2, K–3* (Levels 4–24), gives students the opportunity to think about and retell the story or information in a nonfiction text they have read. Students are asked to start at the beginning and tell what happened in the story or what the author said about the topic. There are specific prompts or questions to use if the student gives a limited retelling or omits important information.

To help you evaluate a student's oral retelling, it is important during the assessment to record as much of the retelling as possible. Underlining on the Story Overview as well as jotting down other information the student includes in the retelling will not only help you make better judgments but will also document why you selected specific descriptors on the Continuum. If you notice during the retelling that it is difficult to underline on the Story Overview, it generally indicates that the student is recalling events out of sequence, misunderstood the story, or is retelling less significant information. It will help when you score if you number the events as they were retold if the student retells them out of sequence. If you tape-record *DRA2* conferences, you may listen again to the retelling if needed.

As you evaluate the student's oral retelling, use what you have underlined and made note of on the Story Overview. On the Continuum, oral retelling is subdivided into the following four areas:

Fiction Texts	Nonfiction Texts
• Sequence of events	• Key ideas and facts
• Characters and details	• Details
• Vocabulary	• Vocabulary
• Teacher support	• Teacher support

Select the descriptor that best reflects the students' performance in each of these four areas. The descriptors selected as Emerging/Intervention or Developing/Instructional indicate what a student needs to learn next in order to give an effective retelling.

To evaluate a student's retelling of fiction texts, note if the retelling includes
- **the important events in sequence**
- **the characters' names**

- **important details**
- **language/vocabulary from the text**

Also consider the number of prompts given after the initial retelling.

To evaluate a student's retelling of nonfiction texts, note if the retelling includes
- **the key ideas and facts**
- **important details**
- **language/vocabulary from the text**

Also consider the number of prompts given after the initial retelling.

CONTINUUM

Select an Advanced performance in the four areas for retelling on the Continuum when
- **the vast majority of the information on the Story Overview is underlined or highlighted in sequential or logical order**
- **the student included the characters' names and important details for fiction texts or all key ideas/facts and important details for non-fiction texts**
- **the student's use of language/vocabulary from the text reflects a good understanding of key words and/or concepts**
- **no prompts were used during the retelling**

Every statement on the overview needs to be included in some fashion in order for the retelling to be considered Advanced.

Select an Independent performance in the four areas in retelling when
- **much of the information on the Story Overview is underlined or highlighted generally in sequential or logical order**
- **most of the characters' names and some important details included by the student are noted**
- **the student's use of language/vocabulary from the text reflects a basic understanding of key words and/or concepts**
- **only one or two prompts were used during the retelling**

Most statements on the overview need to be included in some fashion in order for the retelling to be considered Independent.

Select a Developing/Instructional performance if the student

- gives a partial retelling
- retells events out of sequence; refers to characters using pronouns
- includes misinterpretation
- uses some language/vocabulary from the text that reflects only some understanding of key words/concepts
- requires three or four prompts during retelling

Select an Emerging/Intervention performance if the student

- gives a limited retelling (1–2 events or details)
- refers to characters using general pronouns
- includes incorrect information
- uses general terms or labels reflecting limited understanding of key words/concepts
- requires five or more prompts during retelling

Note that no examples of students' oral retellings have been included at this time.

Nonfiction Text Features: Description

In the *DRA2, K–3*, nonfiction text features include the book title, table of contents, headings, boldfaced words within the text, glossary, labels, captions, and information presented graphically in charts, graphs, maps, diagrams, and timelines. Developing readers are in the process of learning to use nonfiction text features to determine how the text is organized and how to access information presented graphically.

Level 16 Nonfiction
Students reading the nonfiction texts at Level 16 are asked to access information from either a chart or timeline.

Levels 28 Nonfiction
Students reading nonfiction texts at Level 28 are asked to tell why the author used an identified heading. They are also asked to tell what information is presented either in a map or in a web.

Level 38 Nonfiction
Students reading a nonfiction text at Level 38 are asked to tell the information presented in either a map or a graph. They are also asked to locate the glossary and tell what an identified word with multiple meanings means in the selected text.

To evaluate students' ability to use nonfiction text features, consider
- **the accuracy of the information they note**
- **the vocabulary, terms, and labels they used as an indication of their level of understanding**
- **specific details included in their responses**
- **how quickly they access the information**

CONTINUUM

Select an Advanced performance on the Continuum if the student gives an accurate response that includes specific details in his or her response.

Select an Independent performance if the student gives an accurate response to the prompts but includes few or no specific details.

For students who give a partial response or a partially correct response, select an Instructional performance on the Continuum. If the student is unsure or cites incorrect information, select an Intervention performance.

Note that students must meet the criteria for Independent or Advanced for both prompts to be considered Independent or Advanced. If he or she only meets part of the criteria, select the previous level descriptor. For example, if the student does not know why the author used a heading but was able to tell you what the map showed, you would select the Instructional descriptor on the Continuum.

The following are examples of students' oral responses for *DRA2* Levels 16, 28, and 38.

Level 16 NF *Animal Homes*

USING NONFICTION TEXT FEATURES	Independent Descriptor:	Advanced Descriptor:
Prompt: Turn to the chart on page 14. Use the chart, and tell me what animals make their homes in the water. How is the rabbit's home different from the squirrel's home on this chart?	Locates and uses information in the chart to accurately respond to both prompts **Student Oral-Response Example:** *Beaver, alligator, and fishes.* *Rabbits live under the ground.* *Squirrels live in trees.*	Quickly locates and uses information in the chart to accurately respond with details to both prompts **Student Oral-Response Example:** *Beavers, alligators, and fish.* *Rabbits live in holes they dig under the ground. Squirrels live in nests they build up high in trees.*

Level 28 NF *Animals Can Help*

NONFICTION TEXT FEATURES	Independent Descriptor:	Advanced Descriptor:
Prompt: Turn to page 2. Why do you think the author put a heading at the top of this page? Turn to the web on page 15. What does this web show you?	Accurate information accessed from text features **Student Response Example:** *To tell you about what you are reading about.* *It shows different ways animals can help people.*	Detailed information accessed from text features **Student Response Example:** *To help people know that this part is about animals that help.* *It shows what animals are service animals and what they do to help people who can't see or move.*

Level 38 NF *Mae Jemison: Shooting for the Stars*

NONFICTION TEXT FEATURES	Independent Descriptor:	Advanced Descriptor:
Prompt: Turn to page 4. Read the map and tell me what this map shows you. Turn to the glossary. What does the word *degrees* mean in this book?	Accurate information accessed from text features **Student Response Example:** *It shows where Mae visited as a young doctor.* *Certification given to students who have completed advanced training or education.*	Detailed information accessed from text features **Student Response Example:** *The map shows you the countries Mae visited as a young doctor. She was in Cuba, Sierra Leone, Liberia, Kenya, and Thailand.* *Certificates given to students who have completed advanced training or education.*

Fiction Text Features: Description

In *DRA2, K–3*, fiction text features include the book title and cover, the illustrations, and the written text. Readers use information from these features to construct tentative ideas about the story, the characters, the setting, and the plot.

Levels 28–38

In this portion of the assessment, Extending readers are asked to use information from the title, the initial illustrations, and the text read aloud to tell what they know so far about two of the main characters.

To evaluate students' ability to use fiction text features, consider

- the accuracy of the information they include in their descriptions of each character
- the vocabulary they use as an indication of their level of understanding
- specific details included in their responses

CONTINUUM

Select an Advanced performance on the Continuum if the student accurately describes each character with at least three specific details. These responses are often literal and reflect information included in the title and/or illustrations.

Select an Independent performance if the student accurately describes each character with at least two specific details. These responses are also literal but include less specific details from the text than an Advanced response.

If student gives a partial response (e.g., describes only one of the characters) or a partially correct response, select an Instructional performance. If the student is unsure or cites incorrect information, select Intervention.

Note that students must meet the criteria for Independent or Advanced for both characters. If he or she only meets part of the criteria, select the previous level descriptor.

The following are sample responses for *DRA2, K–3*, Levels 28 and 38.

Level 28 F *Missing Sneakers*

USE OF TEXT FEATURES	Independent Descriptor:	Advanced Descriptor:
Prompt: Think about the title, the pictures you have seen, and what you have read so far. Tell me what you know about Sara and Sneakers.	Description of each character; includes at least 2 specific details **Student Response Example:** Sara: *Sara is moving. She has a black cat named Sneakers.* Sneakers: *He likes to go outside.*	Description of each character; includes at least 3 specific details **Student Response Example:** Sara: *Sara is a little girl. She is packing boxes to move. She has to take care of her cat.* Sneakers: *He likes to sneak outside. He is black with white paws.*

Level 38 F *Trouble at the Beaver Pond*

USE OF TEXT FEATURES	Independent Descriptor:	Advanced Descriptor:
Prompt: Think about the title, the pictures you have seen, and what you have read so far. Tell me what you know about the mother beaver and her kits.	Description of each character; includes at least 2 specific details **Student Response Example:** Mother Beaver: *The mother beaver is working on the dam. She is watching her babies.* Kits: *The kits are play fighting. They are on land.*	Description of each character; includes at least 3 specific details. **Student Response Example:** Mother Beaver: *The mother beaver used her big tail and strong front paws to work on the dam. She likes her kits to stay close.* Kits: *The brother and sister kits are playing on the land. They move more quickly in water.*

Making Connections: Description

Making connections with what one reads enhances the reader's understanding of, and at times appreciation for, a text. Connections to self, the world, and other texts support higher-level thinking, such as predicting, interpreting, comparing, contrasting, and evaluating. It also makes a text more memorable. Early and Transitional readers reading *DRA2* Levels 4–16 tell you what a text makes them think of or what connections they made as they read.

To evaluate students' ability to make connections, consider

- **the type and level of the connection**
- **if the connection made reflects a deeper understanding, a basic understanding, or a limited understanding of what was read**

Select an Advanced performance on the Continuum if the student makes a thoughtful connection that reflects a deeper understanding of the text. These responses may include text-to-self or text-to-text connections. They generally include specific details.

Select an Independent performance if the student makes a literal connection reflecting a basic understanding. These responses most frequently are text-to-self connections and may include one or two details.

For students who cite similar objects or actions given in the text, such as "my umbrella" or "when I skate" for their connection, select a Developing/Instructional performance on the Continuum. These types of connections often reflect a limited understanding of the story or text.

When students name an object or event in the text and do not personalize it, such as "food" or "playing," make an unrelated connection, or cannot think of anything, select an Emerging/Intervention performance.

Use the following student examples of oral responses as an initial basis for your evaluation of students' ability to make connections.

Level 4 F *Where Is My Hat?*

MAKING CONNECTIONS	Independent Descriptor: Makes a literal connection that reflects a basic understanding of the story	Advanced Descriptor: Makes a thoughtful connection that reflects a deeper understanding of the story
Prompt: What did this story make you think of? or What connections did you make while reading this story?	Student Oral-Response Example: *It reminded me of when I couldn't find my ball.*	Student Oral-Response Example: *It made me think of when I lost My Little Pony and found it under my bed.*

Level 10 F *Grandma's Surprise*

MAKING CONNECTIONS	Independent Descriptor: Makes a literal connection that reflects a basic understanding of the story	Advanced Descriptor: Makes a thoughtful connection that reflects a deeper understanding of the story
Prompt: What did this story make you think of? or What connections did you make while reading this story?	Student Oral-Response Example: *When I do things with my mom for my dad*	Student Oral-Response Example: *I made a surprise call for dad's birthday. We got a cake for him and he didn't know it. He was in Costa Rica so we celebrated with the surprise cake when he got home.*

Level 16 NF *Animal Homes*

MAKING CONNECTIONS	Independent Descriptor: Makes a literal connection that reflects a basic understanding of the text	Advanced Descriptor: Makes a thoughtful connection that reflects a deeper understanding of the text
Prompt: What did this book make you think of? or What connections did you make while reading this book?	Student Oral-Response Example: *About a bird that made a nest in my tree*	Student Oral-Response Example: *Other animal homes they didn't mention like bees in hives and turtles in water and their shells*

Summary: Description

The Scaffolded Summary in *DRA2, K–3*, gives students reading text Levels 28–38 an opportunity to compose a summary that reflects their level of understanding of what they have read. It is assumed that these Extending readers are able to effectively retell what they have read orally. Unlike an oral retelling that includes most of the information from a text, summaries are not expected to be as long or as detailed as a retelling. Note that students may use the book as they construct their summaries.

Levels 28–38

The summary page in the Student Booklets for *DRA2*, Levels 28–38 scaffolds students' summaries by including transitional words/phrases (e.g., *In the beginning, next, after that*) for stories and main headings in nonfiction texts. In a scaffolded summary, students first determine the important ideas and details within the text, and then use the provided transitional words/phrases or headings to organize their thoughts and write what they think is most important for others to know about the story or topic.

Level 40

At Level 40 students are prompted to include the important characters, events, facts, and details from the beginning, middle, and end of the story or non-fiction text. The summary page in the Student Booklets does not include transitional words/phrases or headings.

To evaluate students' summaries, read for or consider only the content. All structural and/or mechanical errors (grammar, punctuation, and/or spelling) should not be factored into your decision, but they can be noted for future instruction.

On the Continuum, scaffolded written summaries are subdivided into the following two areas: the scaffolded summary and the vocabulary included in the written summary. You are to select the descriptor that best reflects the student's performance in each of these two areas on the Continuum:

- **For fiction texts, students are expected to use the transitional words/phrases to write a one-page summary that includes the major events from the beginning, middle, and end, the characters' names, important details, and**

language/vocabulary from the text that reflects at least a basic understanding of key words/concepts.
- **For nonfiction texts, students are expected to use the headings to write a one-page summary that includes the major ideas with supporting facts, important details, and key vocabulary from the text that reflects at least a basic understanding of key words/concepts.**

Select an Advanced performance in the two areas for summary on the Continuum if the summary

- **is generally written in the students' own words**
- **includes all the important events from the beginning, middle, and end**
- **includes all the important characters' names and important details**
- **includes language/vocabulary from the text that reflects a good understanding of key words and/or concepts**

Select an Independent performance in the two areas for summary if the summary

- **is generally written in the students' own words**
- **includes many of the important events from the beginning, middle, and end**
- **includes important characters' names and some details**
- **includes language/vocabulary from the text that reflects a basic understanding of key words and/or concepts**

If the summary does not reflect at least a basic understanding, determine if it is a partial (Instructional response) or very limited (Intervention response) summary.

- **The Instructional summaries may include misinterpretation.**
- **The Intervention summaries may include incorrect information.**

When there is a significant amount of incorrect information, the summary is to be scored as Intervention even though the student has written a lot or included other accurate information. This student needs to learn how to monitor his or her comprehension and use fix-up strategies when the meaning is not clear.

The descriptors selected at Instructional or Intervention indicate what students need to learn next in order to construct a more effective written summary.

Use the student examples of written responses included in this Teacher Guide for the *DRA2, K–3,* texts you are using as an initial basis for your evaluation of students' written summaries. You will find after you read five to six summaries of the same text, you will be able to select the appropriate descriptor more quickly. It may also help if initially you summarize the text yourself, jotting down what you think is important.

Literal Comprehension: Description

The ability to recall, locate, and use specific information stated in a text enables readers to respond to literal comprehension questions as well as support opinions and justify responses. Literal comprehension also provides the basis for making predictions, inferences, and connections.

Students reading *DRA2* text Levels 28–40 locate and use information explicitly stated in the text to respond to a prompt in the Student Booklet.

To evaluate students' literal comprehension, consider
- **the accuracy of the information**
- **the amount of detail included in the response**

Advanced responses include accurate detailed information. Independent responses also include accurate information but generally only a few details. Partial or partially correct responses are scored as Instructional. Incorrect responses and no response are scored as Intervention.

Use the student examples of the written responses included for the *DRA2* texts as an initial basis for your evaluation of students' responses. Note that students may copy directly from the text to respond to literal prompts or questions and that their responses may vary and still be accurate.

Interpretation: Description

The ability to go beyond the literal meaning of a text enables readers to gain a deeper understanding as they use prior knowledge to grasp the meaning of what is implied by the author.

In the Interpretation section of *DRA2, K–3,* students reading Levels 18–40 use critical-thinking skills to answer questions that require them to infer beyond the literal information given in the text. Students either tell or write about what they think was implied in the text in response to a question or prompt.

To evaluate students' ability to make inferences, consider
- **how well they understand important text implications**
- **what supporting details are included in their response**

Select an Advanced performance on the Continuum if students demonstrated insightful understanding of important text implications and included supporting details in their response.

Select an Independent performance if students understood important text implications and included some supporting details. The difference between an Independent and an Advanced performance is that Advanced is more thoughtful, goes deeper, and/or connects more details within the story.

If students' interpretation only reflects some understanding of the important text implications and includes few or no supporting details, select an Instructional performance. Often these responses are more literal or include misinterpretation. You often have to infer students' intended meaning.

When students do not respond or demonstrate little understanding of important text implications, select an Intervention performance. These responses are often based on incorrect information.

Use the student examples of the oral responses below or written responses starting on page 88 as an initial basis for your evaluation of students' ability to interpret/make inferences.

Level 18 F *Game Day*		
INTERPRETATION **Prompt:** What do you think the author is trying to tell you in this story?	**Independent Descriptor:** Understands important text implications; may include supporting details **Student Oral-Response Example:** *That it is good to be helpful and a #1 friend.*	**Advanced Descriptor:** Insightful understanding of important text implications with supporting details or rationale **Student Oral-Response Example:** *Since Raccoon learned that helping friends can be good, you should always be proud of yourself for helping people.*

Level 20 F *Green Freddie*		
INTERPRETATION **Prompt:** What do you think the author is trying to tell you in this story?	**Independent Descriptor:** Understands important text implications; may include supporting details **Student Oral-Response Example:** *Everybody doesn't have to look or be the same. It's okay to be different.*	**Advanced Descriptor:** Insightful understanding of important text implications with supporting details or rationale **Student Oral-Response Example:** *It doesn't matter about your skin color. You can be glad what color you are, like white people and black people.*

Reflection: Description

Readers use their prior knowledge to help them determine the importance of, reflect on, and evaluate what they read. Students' abilities to establish and/or use criteria when making judgments are important skills in critical reading and thinking. In *DRA2, K–3*, students reading Levels 18–40 identify what they think is the most significant event or message in a text and give reason(s) for their opinion. The ability to justify one's response is an important skill for all readers/learners. It enables others to know the basis for a decision and provides an opening for further discussion.

To evaluate students' ability to reflect and identify significant events and/or messages, consider
- **Did this student identify a significant event or message?**
- **Did he or she give at least a relevant reason for his or her opinion?**

Select an Advanced performance on the Continuum if the student identifies a significant message/event and gives reason(s) for his or her opinion that demonstrates higher-level thinking. When identifying the most important event, Advanced students generally understand that a chain of events leads to the resolution or conclusion. They often identify the initial or at least an earlier event in the story as most important. When identifying the most important message, they are able to synthesize information from the text and prior knowledge to relay a significant message.

Select an Independent performance if the student identifies a significant message/event and gives a relevant reason(s) for his or her opinion. At times, these responses identify the same event or message as students give for Advanced. The difference is in the reason given. The reason is relevant but does not reflect higher-level or more in-depth thinking.

Select an Instructional performance if the student identifies a less significant message/event and gives a general reason for his or her opinion.

When students do not respond or identify an unrelated message/event and/or give no reason for their opinion, select an Intervention performance. These responses are often based on incorrect information.

Use the student examples of the oral responses below or the written responses starting on page 88 as an initial basis for your evaluation of students' level of performance for Reflection.

Level 18 F *Game Day*

REFLECTION	Independent Descriptor:	Advanced Descriptor:
Prompt: 1. What do you think was the most important thing that happened in this story? 2. Why do you think that was important?	Identifies a significant event _and_ gives relevant reason(s) for opinion **Student Oral-Response Example:** 1. *That all the animals got a medal, no one got left out.* 2. *No one was sad.*	Identifies a significant event _and_ gives reason(s) for opinion that reflects higher-level thinking **Student Oral-Response Example:** 1. *Raccoon's friends gave her a medal. Then she knew she was a good friend.* 2. *Because she had been sad but now she was happy and proud.*

Level 20 F *Green Freddie*

REFLECTION	Independent Descriptor:	Advanced Descriptor:
Prompt: 1. What do you think was the most important thing that happened in this story? 2. Why do you think that was important?	Identifies a significant event _and_ gives relevant reason(s) for opinion **Student Oral-Response Example:** 1. *The wise owl helped the frog see that green was a good color to be.* 2. *Because he was being kind to Freddie.*	Identifies a significant event _and_ gives reason(s) for opinion that reflects higher-level thinking **Student Oral-Response Example:** 1. *When the owl came to help Freddie.* 2. *The owl helped him understand people or animals could be different colors and that's okay.*

Comprehension

Examples of Student Written Responses (Levels 28–40)

This section of the Handbook provides examples of Independent and Advanced written student responses to the Comprehension questions and prompts in the Student Booklet for each Benchmark Assessment Book in Levels 28–40.

Level 28 NF *Animals Can Help*		
PREDICTION **Prompt:** Open the book to the title and table of contents page. What are 3 questions you think may be answered as you read this book?	**Independent Descriptor:** At least 2 reasonable questions that go beyond page(s) read aloud **Student Response Example:** 1. *What are service animals?* 2. *Why do they need animals in nursing homes?*	**Advanced Descriptor:** 3 thoughtful questions that go beyond page(s) read aloud **Student Response Example:** 1. *What do service animals do?* 2. *How do they train them?* 3. *How do service animals help people?*
NONFICTION TEXT FEATURES **Prompt:** 1. Turn to page 2. Why do you think the author put a heading at the top of this page? 2. Turn to the web on page 15. What does this web show you?	**Independent Descriptor:** Accurate information accessed from text features **Student Response Example:** 1. *To tell you about what you are reading about.* 2. *It shows different ways animals can help people.*	**Advanced Descriptor:** Detailed information accessed from text features **Student Response Example:** 1. *To help people know that this part is about animals that help.* 2. *It shows what animals are service animals and what they do to help people who can't see or move.*
SCAFFOLDED SUMMARY **Prompt:** Write 2 important facts in your own words for each heading. You may use the book to help you.	**Independent Descriptor:** Summary in own language; includes important ideas <u>and</u> a few supporting facts from each section (See student response example on next page.)	**Advanced Descriptor:** Summary in own language; includes the most important ideas <u>and</u> some facts from each section (See student response example on next page.)

SCAFFOLDED SUMMARY: VOCABULARY **Prompt:** Write 2 important facts in your own words for each heading. You may use the book to help you.	**Independent Descriptor:** Most language/vocabulary from the text; basic understanding of most key words/concepts **Student Response Example:** Animal Helpers: *Help people who can't see. Some make people laugh and make them feel better.* Service Animals: *Help people who can't move, see, or hear.* Dogs: *Help people who cannot hear.* Monkeys: *Help people do stuff when they can't move.* Horses: *Help people walk down stairs.*	**Advanced Descriptor:** All important language/vocabulary from the text; good understanding of key words/concepts **Student Response Example:** Animal Helpers: *Some animals can help you feel better. Some animals help people move and get stronger.* Service Animals: *Service animals are trained to help people who can't see, hear, or move.* Dogs: *Trained dogs help people who can't hear. When they hear a sound they touch their owner.* Monkeys: *Monkeys help people who can't move. A monkey follows its owner's commands.* Horses: *A horse wears a special harness. It helps people walk.*
LITERAL COMPREHENSION **Prompt:** List 2 ways animals help in hospitals and nursing homes.	**Independent Descriptor:** Accurate response **Student Response Example:** *They make people feel more at home and they make them laugh.*	**Advanced Descriptor:** Accurate response with specific details **Student Response Example:** *They help sick people laugh when they do tricks. Petting the animals make people move and use their hands.*
INTERPRETATION **Prompt:** Why do you think a dog must be trained before it can help someone who cannot see?	**Independent Descriptor:** Understands important text implications; may include supporting details **Student Response Example:** *It won't know what to do. It might lead the person into a busy road.*	**Advanced Descriptor:** Insightful understanding of important text implications with supporting details or rationale **Student Response Example:** *If the dog is not trained it won't know how to help. They need to learn how to lead them across streets and up and down stairs so their owners are safe.*
REFLECTION **Prompt:** What do you think is the most important thing you learned from reading this book? Tell why you think it is important.	**Independent Descriptor:** Significant message and a relevant reason for opinion **Student Response Example:** *I learned that dogs and cats visit people in nursing homes. That's important because they make old people smile.*	**Advanced Descriptor:** Significant message and reason for opinion that reflects higher-level thinking **Student Response Example:** *I learned how monkeys help people who can't move. I think that is important because monkeys can do things for them that they can't do anymore by themselves and they are more like you and me.*

Student Written Responses

PREDICTION **Prompt:** Open the book to the title and table of contents page. What are 3 questions you think may be answered as you read this book?	**Independent Descriptor:** At least 2 reasonable questions that go beyond page(s) read aloud **Student Response Example:** *1. How can you make peanut butter?* *2. How do you get the peanuts from the plants?*	**Advanced Descriptor:** 3 thoughtful questions that go beyond page(s) read aloud **Student Response Example:** *1. How is peanut butter made in the factory?* *2. How do they make crunchy and smooth?* *3. How are peanuts gathered?*
NONFICTION TEXT FEATURES **Prompt:** 1. Turn to page 4. Why do you think the author put a heading at the top of this page? 2. Now read the map, and tell me what it shows you.	**Independent Descriptor:** Accurate information accessed from text features **Student Response Example:** *1. So if someone wants to know about growing peanuts they look on this page.* *2. Shows where in U.S. peanuts are grown.*	**Advanced Descriptor:** Detailed information accessed from text features **Student Response Example:** *1. It tells you that this part tells you about growing peanuts.* *2. You know which of the states in the US peanuts grow. Yellow shows where peanuts are grown. Green parts are where peanuts are not grown.*
SCAFFOLDED SUMMARY **SCAFFOLDED SUMMARY: VOCABULARY** **Prompt:** Write 2 important facts in your own words for each heading. You may use the book to help you.	**Independent Descriptor:** Summary in own language; includes important ideas <u>and</u> a few supporting facts from each section **Independent Descriptor:** Most language/vocabulary from the text; basic understanding of most key words/concepts **Student Response Example:** Growing Peanuts: *Peanuts are grown at farms. They come through the soil after two weeks.* Gathering Peanuts: *A digger digs them up in the fall.* Making Peanut Butter: *They are ground one time to make chunky and two times to make smooth.* Peanut Butter Treats: *You can eat peanut butter on different foods.*	**Advanced Descriptor:** Summary in own language; includes the most important ideas <u>and</u> some supporting facts from each section **Advanced Descriptor:** All important language/vocabulary from the text; good understanding of key words/concepts **Student Response Example:** Growing Peanuts: *Peanuts grow on farms where it is warm. Peanuts grow in sandy soil.* Gathering Peanuts: *Peanuts are dug up by machine called digger. After two or three days the peanuts are dried and picked up.* Making Peanut Butter: *They are roasted. For chunky peanut butter peanuts are ground once. They are ground twice for creamy.* Peanut Butter Treats: *Peanut butter can be in ice cream and cookies. It is good for you.*

LITERAL COMPREHENSION	Independent Descriptor: Accurate response	Advanced Descriptor: Accurate response with specific details
Prompt: List 2 reasons that most peanuts are grown in the southern part of the United States.	**Student Response Example:** Peanuts grow well in the South because... *1. The soil is sandy.* *2. The weather is warm.*	**Student Response Example:** Peanuts grow well in the South because... *1. Peanuts grow in rich, sandy soil.* *2. They need warm days and nights to grow.*
INTERPRETATION	Independent Descriptor: Understands important text implications; may include supporting details	Advanced Descriptor: Insightful understanding of important text implications with supporting details or rationale
Prompt: Why do you think people use machines to gather peanuts and make peanut butter?	**Student Response Example:** *It's too much work for humans to do.*	**Student Response Example:** *Because it's harder to do it by hand. It is easier and quicker when machines do it.*
REFLECTION	Independent Descriptor: Significant message and a relevant reason for opinion	Advanced Descriptor: Significant message and reason for opinion that reflects higher-level thinking
Prompt: What do you think is the most important thing you learned from reading this book? Tell why you think it is important.	**Student Response Example:** *How they made peanut butter because I was wondering how to make it.*	**Student Response Example:** *I learned that peanut butter is good for you. It gives you energy. That's important because now when I eat peanut butter I know it is good for me.*

Student Written Responses

Level 28 F *Missing Sneakers*

Student Written Responses

USE OF TEXT FEATURES	Independent Descriptor:	Advanced Descriptor:
Prompt: Think about the title, the pictures you have seen, and what you have read so far. Tell me what you know about Sara and Sneakers.	Description of each character; includes at least 2 specific details **Student Response Example:** Sara: *Sara is moving. She has a black cat named Sneakers.* Sneakers: *He likes to go outside.*	Description of each character; includes at least 3 specific details **Student Response Example:** Sara: *Sara is a little girl. She is packing boxes to move. She has to take care of her cat Sneakers.* Sneakers: *He likes to sneak outside. He is black with white paws.*
PREDICTION **Prompt:** What are 3 things you think might happen in the rest of this story?	Independent Descriptor: At least 2 reasonable predictions that go beyond the text read aloud **Student Response Example:** 1. *Sneakers might get lost during the move.* 2. *They might find him back at the old house.*	Advanced Descriptor: 3 thoughtful predictions that go beyond the text read aloud **Student Response Example:** 1. *Sneakers is going to get lost.* 2. *Sara might find him up in the tree.* 3. *Sneakers might get left behind and Sara will be upset.*
SCAFFOLDED SUMMARY	Independent Descriptor: Summary in own language; includes important characters, many of the important events, and some details from the beginning, middle, and end	Advanced Descriptor: Summary in own language; includes all important characters, events, and details from the beginning, middle, and end
SCAFFOLDED SUMMARY: VOCABULARY **Prompt:** Write a summary of this story in your own words. Include the important characters, events, and details. You may use the book and the words below to help you write your summary.	Independent Descriptor: Most language/vocabulary from the text; basic understanding of most key words/concepts **Student Response Example:** In the beginning: *There's a family and a cat and they were moving to a new house with their cat Sneakers.* Next: *So the mother told Sara that they were moving so she had to put her cat in a crate.* Then: *The next morning it was time to go but Sara didn't put her cat in the cat crate.* After that: *Sneakers was gone then she look all over the house and she ask all of the moving men.* In the end: *Then she look outside and in the back yard. Then she heard jingle ball and she look in the moving truck. Then she found her cat.*	Advanced Descriptor: All important language/vocabulary from the text; good understanding of key words/concepts **Student Response Example:** In the beginning: *Sara and Sneakers were going to move from their old house to a new house.* Next: *Sara's mom said to put Sneakers in his crate first thing in the morning. Sneakers loved to sneak out.* Then: *Sara heard the moving truck. She went downstairs to see what the moving men were doing. She forgot to put Sneakers back in his crate.* After that: *Sara went back to her room. When she got to her room she realized Sneakers was gone.* In the end: *She looked everywhere till she heard a jingling noise and looked in the moving truck and found Sneakers in a box. Then they went to the new house.*

LITERAL COMPREHENSION	Independent Descriptor: Accurate response	Advanced Descriptor: Accurate response with specific details
Prompt: List 2 places where Sara looked for Sneakers.	**Student Response Example:** *1. in the den* *2. under some bushes.*	**Student Response Example:** *1. in the cupboards in the kitchen* *2. up a tree in the backyard.*
INTERPRETATION	Independent Descriptor: Understands important text implications; may include supporting details	Advanced Descriptor: Insightful understanding of important text implications with supporting details or rationale
Prompt: What do you think Sara learned?	**Student Response Example:** *To keep an eye on Sneakers and put Sneakers inside his crate when her mother told her.*	**Student Response Example:** *Sara learned that watching Sneakers is very important because she didn't want another pet. He was very special to her.*
REFLECTION	Independent Descriptor: Significant event and a relevant reason for opinion	Advanced Descriptor: Significant event and reason for opinion that reflects higher-level thinking
Prompt: What do you think is the most important event in this story? Tell why you think it is important.	**Student Response Example:** *When Sara heard the jingling noise in the box.* *Because that's how she found Sneakers.*	**Student Response Example:** *When Sara found her cat, Sneakers. Because that's the only pet that she has and if she didn't find him and had to leave she would be very sad.*

USE OF TEXT FEATURES **Prompt:** Think about the title, the pictures you have seen, and what you have read so far. Tell me what you know about Little Skunk and Little Rabbit.	**Independent Descriptor:** Description of each character; includes at least 2 specific details **Student Response Example:** Little Skunk: *His mother said Little Skunk is beautiful. Little Skunk is happy.* Little Rabbit: *Little Rabbit said Little Skunk is not beautiful.*	**Advanced Descriptor:** Description of each character; includes at least 3 specific details **Student Response Example:** Little Skunk: *I know that Mother Skunk thinks Little Skunk is beautiful. Little Skunk has shiny fur. He's happy and ran off to tell the other animals.* Little Rabbit: *Little Rabbit has long ears and a short tail. He does not think Little Skunk is beautiful.*
PREDICTION **Prompt:** What are 3 things you think might happen in the rest of this story?	**Independent Descriptor:** At least 2 reasonable predictions that go beyond the text read aloud **Student Response Example:** 1. *Everyone is going to say Baby Skunk is not beautiful.* 2. *Mother Skunk might get mad and tell his friends to go away.*	**Advanced Descriptor:** 3 thoughtful predictions that go beyond the text read aloud **Student Response Example:** 1. *Little Skunk might meet other animals that think he's not pretty just like Little Rabbit said.* 2. *Little Skunk might think to himself that he is really ugly.* 3. *At the end a snake might tell him, "Do you think I'm ugly because someone else said I'm ugly?" And the snake might say don't believe them.*
SCAFFOLDED SUMMARY	**Independent Descriptor:** Summary in own language; includes important characters, many of the important events, and some details from the beginning, middle, and end (See student response example on next page.)	**Advanced Descriptor:** Summary in own language; includes all important characters, events, and details from the beginning, middle, and end (See student response example on next page.)

Student Written Responses

SCAFFOLDED SUMMARY: VOCABULARY	Independent Descriptor:	Advanced Descriptor:
Prompt: Write a summary of this story in your own words. Include the important characters, events, and details. You may use the book and the words below to help you write your summary. In the beginning, Next, Then, After that, In the end,	Most language/vocabulary from the text; basic understanding of most key words/concepts **Student Response Example:** In the beginning: *Mother Skunk said that Little Skunk was beautiful he was so happy he ran in the forest.* Next: *He met a rabbit he said his tail was too long his ears they were too tiny.* Then: *He met a deer he said that his legs were too short.* After that: *He met a snake he said he much too fat and you don't have pretty designs.* In the end: *Mother Skunk said everything was beautiful in its own way.*	All important language /vocabulary from the text; good understanding of key words/concepts **Student Response Example:** In the beginning: *His mother said that he was beautiful. And when his mother said that she thought he was beautiful and he was happy about it.* Next: *He went to the forest and told Rabbit that his mother said that he was beautiful. And Rabbit said that he wasn't.* Then: *He ran into a deer and he said that his mom said that he was beautiful. And the deer said that he wasn't.* After that: *He ran into a snake and he said what his mother said he was beautiful. But snake said no he wasn't.* In the end: *He ran home and he told his mother what they said about him that he wasn't beautiful after all. But his mother explained to him that everybody is different. Little Skunk touched the tree and rock. He said everything in the woods is beautiful.*
LITERAL COMPREHENSION **Prompt:** List 2 reasons why Little Deer did not think Little Skunk was beautiful.	Independent Descriptor: Accurate response **Student Response Example:** *1. He is small.* *2. His legs are short.*	Advanced Descriptor: Accurate response with specific details **Student Response Example:** *1. Little Skunk was small for an animal.* *2. He can't run very fast with his short legs.*
INTERPRETATION **Prompt:** What do you think Little Skunk learned?	Independent Descriptor: Understands important text implications; may include supporting details **Student Response Example:** *He learned all the animals can be beautiful.*	Advanced Descriptor: Insightful understanding of important text implications with important supporting details or rationale **Student Response Example:** *I think he learned that everything can be beautiful but in different ways.*
REFLECTION **Prompt:** What do you think is the most important event in this story? Tell why you think it is important.	Independent Descriptor: Significant event and a relevant reason for opinion **Student Response Example:** *When he learned everything is beautiful. Because everything is beautiful in its own way.*	Advanced Descriptor: Significant event and reason for opinion that reflects higher-level thinking **Student Response Example:** *When the Mother Skunk gave Little Skunk the example of the tree and the rock because then the Little Skunk thinks he's beautiful like the other animals—even though he is different.*

Student Written Responses

USE OF TEXT FEATURES	**Independent Descriptor:**	**Advanced Descriptor:**
Prompt: Think about the title, the pictures, and what you have read so far. Tell me what you know about Pedro and Ann.	Description of each character; includes at least 2 specific details **Student Response Example:** Pedro: *Ann and Pedro are friends. They are nice kids.* Ann: *Ann plays every afternoon at Pedro's house. She wants a dog.*	Description of each character; includes at least 3 specific details **Student Response Example:** Pedro: *Pedro plays with Ann almost every afternoon. They help Miss Clark.* Ann: *Ann wants a dog but her brother is allergic to them. Ann plays with Zane, Miss Clark's dog.*
PREDICTION **Prompt:** What are 3 things you think might happen in the rest of this story?	**Independent Descriptor:** At least 2 reasonable predictions that go beyond the text read aloud **Student Response Example:** *1. They will help Mrs. Clark more.* *2. I think Miss Clark's leg will get better.*	**Advanced Descriptor:** 3 thoughtful predictions that go beyond the text read aloud **Student Response Example:** *1. I think Miss Clark will get better.* *2. Pedro and Ann might do a really good job helping since its called Busy Helpers.* *3. Miss Clark will be happy that Pedro and Ann are helping.*
SCAFFOLDED SUMMARY	**Independent Descriptor:** Summary in own language; includes important characters, many of the important events, and some details from the beginning, middle, and end	**Advanced Descriptor:** Summary in own language; includes all important characters, events, and details from the beginning, middle, and end
SCAFFOLDED SUMMARY: VOCABULARY **Prompt:** Write a summary of this story in your own words. Include the important characters, events, and details. You may use the book and the words below to help you write your summary. In the beginning, Next, Then, After that, In the end,	**Independent Descriptor:** Most language/vocabulary from the text; basic understanding of most key words/concepts **Student Response Example:** In the beginning: *Most afternoons Ann and Pedro played in the back yard at Pedro's house.* Next: *Miss Clark broke her leg.* Then: *Ann and Pedro started to help Miss Clark.* After that: *They went to the store and lost Zane and were looking for him.* In the end: *They told Miss Clark what happened and then Miss Clark said it's ok because Zane came back. They were all happy.*	**Advanced Descriptor:** All important language/vocabulary from the text; good understanding of key words/concepts **Student Response Example:** In the beginning: *Pedro and Ann are helping Miss Clark because she broke her leg.* Next: *Miss Clark gives the kids odd jobs. They do a good job pulling weeds and taking care of Zane.* Then: *Miss Clark said "can you kids get some groceries and walk Zane?" Miss Clark said "do not leave Zane alone."* After that: *They walked Zane to the store. Ann went into the grocery looking for Pedro. Ann left Zane alone and he ran away. They were upset and looked everywhere.* In the end: *They found him at Miss Clark's house and they promised never to leave him alone again.*

LITERAL COMPREHENSION	**Independent Descriptor:** Accurate response	**Advanced Descriptor:** Accurate response with specific details
Prompt: List 3 ways that Pedro and Ann helped Miss Clark.	**Student Response Example:** *1. Walked Zane* *2. Washed dishes* *3. Got groceries*	**Student Response Example:** *1. Pedro washed the dishes.* *2. Ann gave Zane a bath.* *3. They pulled weeds from the yard.*
INTERPRETATION	**Independent Descriptor:** Understands important text implications; may include supporting details	**Advanced Descriptor:** Insightful understanding of important text implications with supporting details or rationale
Prompt: Why do you think Miss Clark said to Pedro and Ann that they would do better next time?	**Student Response Example:** *Now they know Zane runs home when he is left alone.*	**Student Response Example:** *They were pretty good. They learned their lesson and lessons make people do better.*
REFLECTION	**Independent Descriptor:** Significant event and a relevant reason for opinion	**Advanced Descriptor:** Significant event and reason for opinion that reflects higher-level thinking
Prompt: 1. What do you think is the most important event in this story? 2. Tell why you think it is important.	**Student Response Example:** *1. When they found Zane at home.* *2. Because he wasn't lost.*	**Student Response Example:** *1. When Pedro and Ann told Miss Clark that they lost Zane.* *2. People don't get into trouble when they tell the truth.*

USE OF TEXT FEATURES **Prompt:** Think about the title, the pictures you have seen, and what you have read so far. Tell me what you know about Karla and Tiger.	**Independent Descriptor:** Description of each character; includes at least 2 specific details **Student Response Example:** Karla: *Karla takes care of her cat. She takes Tiger in the house.* Tiger: *Tiger the cat doesn't like storms or water.*	**Advanced Descriptor:** Description of each character; includes at least 3 specific details **Student Response Example:** Karla: *I know that Karla is very anxious about Tiger. Karla is very helpful. I know that she helped her dad carry the chairs into the garage to get ready for the storm.* Tiger: *Tiger does not like wind or water. He is a scaredy-cat.*
PREDICTION **Prompt:** What are 3 things you think might happen in the rest of this story?	**Independent Descriptor:** At least 2 reasonable predictions that go beyond the text read aloud **Student Response Example:** 1. *The lights go out.* 2. *Tiger gets scared and runs away.*	**Advanced Descriptor:** 3 thoughtful predictions that go beyond the text read aloud. **Student Response Example:** 1. *Tiger will get lost in the wind and rain.* 2. *Karla might be sad because Tiger is not there.* 3. *They'll find him at the end and they'll be happy.*
SCAFFOLDED SUMMARY	**Independent Descriptor:** Summary in own language; includes important characters, many of the important events, and some details from the beginning, middle, and end	**Advanced Descriptor:** Summary in own language; includes all important characters, events, and details from the beginning, middle, and end
SCAFFOLDED SUMMARY: VOCABULARY **Prompt:** Write a summary of this story in your own words. Include the important characters, events, and details. You may use the book and the words below to help you write your summary. In the beginning, Next, Then, After that, In the end,	**Independent Descriptor:** Most language/vocabulary from the text; basic understanding of most key words/concepts **Student Response Example:** In the beginning: *Karla had a cat. She helped her dad get the chairs so they don't break in the storm.* Next: *Mom got candles and flashlights in case the lights go out.* Then: *Karla was watching TV and she was with her cat Tiger. Thunder made the lights go out. The wind opened the door and Tiger went out.* After that: *She asked if she could go out. It's too dangerous. They said Tiger would hide.* In the end: *The storm ends. Karla finds Tiger under the porch.*	**Advanced Descriptor:** All important language/vocabulary from the text; good understanding of key words/concepts **Student Response Example:** In the beginning: *Karla was helping Dad. Mom was getting candles and flashlights ready. There was a storm coming. Karla finds Tiger hiding.* Next: *They watched about the storm on the news. All of a sudden, a tree tipped on the wires. The power went out.* Then: *Wind pushed the door open. Papers and books blew out the door. Karla thinks Tiger ran outside.* After that: *Her parents won't let her go outside to look for Tiger. They try to cheer her up by telling stories.* In the end: *After the storm blew over they looked outside. Karla found Tiger under the porch. He was sopping wet. He wasn't scared.*

LITERAL COMPREHENSION	Independent Descriptor:	Advanced Descriptor:
Prompt: List 3 things that happened when something crashed against Karla's house during the storm.	Accurate response **Student Response Example:** *1. Tiger ran away from Karla.* *2. The lights went out.* *3. TV went out.*	Accurate response with specific details **Student Response Example:** *1. Tiger jumped off Karla's lap and ran away.* *2. All the lights went out.* *3. The refrigerator and the TV stopped working.*
INTERPRETATION **Prompt:** Why do you think Karla said Tiger had a whirlwind of a day?	**Independent Descriptor:** Understands important text implications; may include supporting details **Student Response Example:** *It's windy when storms happen and Tiger was out in the storm.*	**Advanced Descriptor:** Insightful understanding of important text implications with supporting details or rationale **Student Response Example:** *Because Tiger got swept up in a whirlwind of papers and books and ended up outside.*
REFLECTION **Prompt:** 1. What do you think is the most important event in this story? 2. Tell why you think it is important.	**Independent Descriptor:** Significant event <u>and</u> a relevant reason for opinion **Student Response Example:** *1. When Karla found Tiger.* *2. Because she was happy he was safe.*	**Advanced Descriptor:** Significant event <u>and</u> reason for opinion that reflects higher-level thinking **Student Response Example:** *1. When Karla kept calling Tiger's name.* *2. Because he came out from the papers under the porch.*

Student Written Responses

USE OF TEXT FEATURES **Prompt:** Think about the title, the pictures you have seen, and what you have read so far. Tell me what you know about Zoe and Sam.	**Independent Descriptor:** Description of each character; includes at least 2 specific details **Student Response Example:** Zoe: *Zoe and Sam are twins.* Sam: *Sam teases Zoe when she lost her bracelet and necklace.*	**Advanced Descriptor:** Description of each character; includes at least 3 specific details **Student Response Example:** Zoe: *Zoe's heart necklace disappears. She uses her necklace when she takes a test.* Sam: *I know that Sam and Zoe are twins and Sam likes to tease Zoe.*
PREDICTION **Prompt:** What are 3 things you think might happen in the rest of this story?	**Independent Descriptor:** At least 2 reasonable predictions that go beyond the text read aloud **Student Response Example:** 1. *I think that Sam is going to miss some things too.* 2. *I think that Zoe and Sam's cat took their things.*	**Advanced Descriptor:** 3 thoughtful predictions that go beyond the text read aloud **Student Response Example:** 1. *Some more things will go missing.* 2. *Sam will keep teasing but will help her find them.* 3. *They will probably find out the mystery.*
SCAFFOLDED SUMMARY	**Independent Descriptor:** Summary in own language; includes important characters, many of the important events, and some details from the beginning, middle, and end	**Advanced Descriptor:** Summary in own language; includes all important characters, events, and details from the beginning, middle, and end
SCAFFOLDED SUMMARY: VOCABULARY **Prompt:** Write a summary of this story in your own words. Include the important characters, events, and details. You may use the book and the words below to help you write your summary. In the beginning, Next, Then, After that, In the end,	**Independent Descriptor:** Most language/vocabulary from the text; basic understanding of most key words/concepts **Student Response Example:** In the beginning: *Zoe's things like her necklace and her bracelet and her pink shoelace are missing.* Next: *Sam lost his pencil, his baseball sock and his toothbrush.* Then: *Before you knew it their dad lost his green striped tie.* After that: *Then they had to get ready for a picture and they needed their cat for the picture.* In the end: *They find Cat and all of their things under the sofa with the cat. The cat had taken all of their stuff.*	**Advanced Descriptor:** All important language/vocabulary from the text; good understanding of key words/concepts **Student Response Example:** In the beginning: *One day at the Mays' house Zoe said I can't find my silver heart. then Sam couldn't find his lucky pencil.* Next: *Dad couldn't find his striped tie and Mom couldn't find her yarn and the knitting needles.* Then: *Aunt Clara came to their house to take a family picture and Zoe said Cat should be in the picture with us.* After that: *They looked in the spots that they knew she liked but she wasn't there. They looked under the sofa and they found Cat.* In the end: *She had Zoe's necklace on her paw. Then the family lifted up the sofa and found all the missing stuff. Cat wasn't getting a lot of time with the family that's why she took the stuff.*

LITERAL COMPREHENSION	Independent Descriptor:	Advanced Descriptor:
Prompt: List 2 things that Zoe and Sam were each missing.	Accurate response **Student Response Example:** Zoe: *shoelace, bracelet* Sam: *lucky pencil, sock*	Accurate response with specific details **Student Response Example:** Zoe: *silver heart necklace, pink shoe lace,* Sam: *lucky pencil, baseball sock*
INTERPRETATION	Independent Descriptor:	Advanced Descriptor:
Prompt: Why do you think Sam and Zoe did not suspect the cat?	Understands important text implications; may include supporting details **Student Response Example:** *I think they did not suspect him because usually a cat would not take things.*	Insightful understanding of important text implications with supporting details or rationale **Student Response Example:** *They didn't think it was Cat because she probably took things when they were gone. She was good when they were home.*
REFLECTION	Independent Descriptor:	Advanced Descriptor:
Prompt: 1. What do you think is the most important event in this story? 2. Tell why you think it is important.	Significant event <u>and</u> a relevant reason for opinion **Student Response Example:** 1. *I think when they got the cat out from under the couch with the chain.* 2. *Because then they found everything.*	Significant event <u>and</u> reason for opinion that reflects higher-level thinking **Student Response Example:** 1. *When Aunt Clara came to take their family picture* 2. *Because when they looked for Cat they found their stuff.*

Student Written Responses

Level 34 F *Summary Discovery*

(heading reads:) Level 34 F *Summer Discovery*

USE OF TEXT FEATURES	**Independent Descriptor:** Description of each character; includes at least 2 specific details	**Advanced Descriptor:** Description of each character; includes at least 3 specific details
Prompt: Think about the title, the pictures you have seen, and what you have read so far. Tell me what you know about Noah and his mom.	**Student Response Example:** Noah: *Noah always gets notes by his mother. Noah likes to collect rocks.* Noah's mom: *Noah's mom works at the hospital.*	**Student Response Example:** Noah: *Noah is at his last day at school. He hides notes from mom. He has a rock collection.* Noah's mom: *His mom works late sometimes at the hospital because his dad died.*
PREDICTION	**Independent Descriptor:** At least 2 reasonable predictions that go beyond the text read aloud	**Advanced Descriptor:** 3 thoughtful predictions that go beyond the text read aloud
Prompt: What are 3 things you think might happen in the rest of this story?	**Student Response Example:** 1. *Noah is going to look for a way not to go to his grandma and grandpa.* 2. *When Noah goes to grandparents he's going to find something cool.*	**Student Response Example:** 1. *Noah might be mad about having to stay with his grandparents in the summer.* 2. *Maybe he'll find more rocks for his collection.* 3. *He will find that is not so bad and he'll like it.*
SCAFFOLDED SUMMARY	**Independent Descriptor:** Summary in own language; includes important characters, many of the important events, and some details from the beginning, middle, and end	**Advanced Descriptor:** Summary in own language; includes all important characters, events, and details from the beginning, middle, and end
SCAFFOLDED SUMMARY: VOCABULARY	**Independent Descriptor:** Most language/vocabulary from the text; basic understanding of most key words/concepts	**Advanced Descriptor:** All important language/vocabulary from the text; good understanding of key words/concepts
Prompt: Write a summary of this story in your own words. Include the important characters, events, and details. You may use the book and the words below to help you write your summary. In the beginning, Next, Then, After that, In the end,	**Student Response Example:** In the beginning: *Noah was just finishing school and was looking forward to a good summer.* Next: *He heard the news that he was going to stay at his grandparent's house and was very mad.* Then: *Noah was having fun when he was reading his book to gramps.* After that: *There was a package for Noah that turned out to be his rock collection.* In the end: *Gramps and Noah found Gramp's rock collection and they decided to build their collections together.*	**Student Response Example:** In the beginning: *Noah was planning to play with friends and go to the pool for summer but his mom wanted him to go to his grandparents' house for the summer.* Next: *Noah's grandmother wanted him to go to the supermarket so he could read the labels on the cans and boxes because his grandfather cannot eat salt.* Then: *His grandfather gave him some old books his dad had but he could not read them so he read to his grandfather* Freckle Juice. After that: *Noah's grandmother ask if he wanted to see a movie with her friend and her grandson he did.* In the end: *Noah's mom sent him his rock collection and after Noah thanked his mother his grandfather showed Noah his rock collection and Noah thought it would be a good summer after all.*

Student Written Responses *(vertical side label)*

LITERAL COMPREHENSION	Independent Descriptor:	Advanced Descriptor:
Prompt: List 3 things that Noah thought about the detective stories Gramps found in the attic.	Accurate response **Student Response Example:** *1. He thought the print was too small.* *2. He thought they looked old and boring.*	Accurate response with specific details **Student Response Example:** *1. Noah thought they would be hard to read.* *2. He thought the pages were old and brown.* *3. The story looked boring.*
INTERPRETATION **Prompt:** What do you think Noah learned?	Independent Descriptor: Understands important text implications; may include supporting details **Student Response Example:** *Sometimes bad things turn out good. Noah and Gramps both liked rocks.*	Advanced Descriptor: Insightful understanding of important text implications with supporting details or rationale **Student Response Example:** *I think Noah learns to wait and see and not think that things will be bad before they happen.*
REFLECTION **Prompt:** 1. What do you think is the most important event in this story? 2. Tell why you think it is important.	Independent Descriptor: Significant event <u>and</u> a relevant reason for opinion **Student Response Example:** *1. When Gramps found his old rock collection in the attic.* *2. Because it made Noah happy.*	Advanced Descriptor: Significant event <u>and</u> reason for opinion that reflects higher-level thinking **Student Response Example:** *1. When Noah finds he has got something in common with Gramps.* *2. Because his summer won't be boring after all.*

Level 38 NF *Mae Jemison: Shooting for the Stars*

PREDICTION

Prompt:

Open the book to the title and table of contents page. What are 3 questions you think may be answered as you read this book?

Independent Descriptor:
At least 2 reasonable questions that go beyond page(s) read aloud
Student Response Example:
1. How was the space training?
2. When was the first space flight?

Advanced Descriptor:
3 thoughtful questions that go beyond page(s) read aloud
Student Response Example:
1. What was Mae's first space training like?
2. What is a Space Lab?
3. How did her dream come true?

NONFICTION TEXT FEATURES

Prompt:
1. Turn to page 4. Read the map and tell me what this map shows you.
2. Turn to the glossary. What does the word *degrees* mean in this book?

Independent Descriptor:
Accurate information accessed from text features
Student Response Example:
1. It shows you where Mae visited as a young doctor.
2. Certification given to students who have completed advanced training or education.

Advanced Descriptor:
Detailed information accessed from text features
Student Response Example:
1. The map shows you the countries Mae visited as a young doctor. She was in Cuba, Sierra Leone, Liberia, Kenya, and Thailand.
2. Certificates given to students who have completed advanced training or education.

SCAFFOLDED SUMMARY

Independent Descriptor:
Summary in own language; includes important ideas <u>and</u> a few supporting facts from each section

Advanced Descriptor:
Summary in own language; includes the most important ideas <u>and</u> some supporting facts from each section

SCAFFOLDED SUMMARY: VOCABULARY

Prompt:
Write a summary of this book in your own words. Include the important ideas and facts. You may use the book and the headings below to help you write your summary.

Mae's Childhood
Mae as a Young Woman
Mae's Space Training
Mae's First Flight in Space
In the Spacelab
A Dream Come True

Independent Descriptor:
Most language/vocabulary from the text; basic understanding of most key words/concepts
Student Response Example:
Mae's Childhood: *When Mae was a kid her dream was to go into space. But she also wanted to be a doctor.*
Mae as a Young Woman: *Mae became a doctor and went around the world. She got back and signed up for the space program.*
Mae's Space Training: *For a whole year she trained. She had to wait four years to go up in space.*
Mae's First Flight in Space: *Mae ate breakfast and changed into her space suit and got into space with the other six people.*
In the Spacelab: *When she was in space she studied about frogs.*
A Dream Come True: *When she got back people had parties for her.*

Advanced Descriptor:
All important language/vocabulary from the text; good understanding of key words/concepts
Student Response Example:
Mae's Childhood: *She wanted to be a scientist and go into space. She lived in Chicago.*
Mae as a Young Woman: *Mae got 2 degrees. She became a doctor and traveled around the world. Then she applied to be an astronaut.*
Mae's Space Training: *She went up in a training jet. She learned how to eat and drink in space. She could float around.*
Mae's First Flight in Space: *In 1992 she worked in the Spacelab. The Endeavour was in space 8 minutes. Her flight took 8 days.*
In the Spacelab: *She saw hurricane Bonnie and Chicago. She watched tadpoles grow into frogs.*
A Dream Come True: *She was the first African American woman in space. Chicago had a party for her when she got back.*

LITERAL COMPREHENSION	Independent Descriptor:	Advanced Descriptor:
Prompt: List 3 things that Mae learned to do in the astronaut training program.	Accurate response **Student Response Example:** 1. She learned how to put on her suit. 2. She learned how to move in space. 3. She learned about the shuttle.	Accurate response with specific details **Student Response Example:** 1. How to eat and drink in space. 2. How to move around while floating in the air. 3. How to work in the space suit.
INTERPRETATION **Prompt:** Why do you think Mae wanted to be an astronaut?	**Independent Descriptor:** Understands important text implications; may include supporting details **Student Response Example:** I think Mae wanted to be an astronaut because she always wanted to see outer space.	**Advanced Descriptor:** Insightful understanding of important text implications with supporting details or rationale **Student Response Example:** I think she wanted to be an astronaut because she wanted to learn about space and to find out ways not to get sick in space.
REFLECTION **Prompt:** 1. What do you think is the most important thing that you learned from this book? 2. Tell why you think it is important.	**Independent Descriptor:** Significant message <u>and</u> a relevant reason for opinion **Student Response Example:** 1. That she was the first African American woman to go into space. 2. She wanted to be and she got what she wanted because she worked hard.	**Advanced Descriptor:** Significant message <u>and</u> reason for opinion that reflects higher-level thinking **Student Response Example:** 1. I thought she had confidence in herself to keep wanting to be a scientist even though it wasn't encouraged. 2. I think it is important because she had to believe in herself no matter what anyone said.

Student Written Responses

Student Written Responses

PREDICTION

Prompt:

Open the book to the title and table of contents page. What are 3 questions you think may be answered as you read this book?

Independent Descriptor:

At least 2 reasonable questions that go beyond page(s) read aloud

Student Response Example:

1. Does he make the baseball team?
2. What is the Great Home Run Race?

Advanced Descriptor:

3 thoughtful questions that go beyond page(s) read aloud

Student Response Example:

1. How many home runs did Sammy hit?
2. Why is he called Slammin Sammy?
3. I wonder if he gets hurt when it says hero on and off the field.

NONFICTION TEXT FEATURES

Prompt:

1. Turn to page 13. Read the graph, and tell me what this graph shows you.
2. Turn to the glossary. What does the word *scouts* mean in this book?

Independent Descriptor:

Accurate information accessed from text features

Student Response Example:

1. It shows how much home runs he did. The home runs Sammy made in June were twenty home runs. In September he made eleven home runs.
2. Scouts mean when people who are sent out to find ball players.

Advanced Descriptor:

Detailed information accessed from text features

Student Response Example:

1. I think he put it in a graph because he wants you to see the numbers clearly. Its easier to understand.
In June he hit 20 and Sept. 11 so he hit 9 more home runs in June.
2. Scouts are people who are sent out to find talented ball players.

SCAFFOLDED SUMMARY

Independent Descriptor:

Summary in own language; includes important ideas <u>and</u> a few supporting facts from each section

Advanced Descriptor:

Summary in own language; includes the important ideas <u>and</u> some supporting facts from each section

SCAFFOLDED SUMMARY: VOCABULARY

Prompt:

Write a summary of this book in your own words. Include the important ideas and facts. You may use the book and the headings below to help you write your summary.

Sammy as a Boy
Sammy Tries Out for a Baseball Team
Sammy Begins to Hit Home Runs
The Great Home Run Race
A Hero on and off the Field

Independent Descriptor:

Most language/vocabulary from the text; basic understanding of most key words/concepts

Student Response Example:

Sammy as a Boy: *When Sammy was a boy he wanted to play baseball but he used a milk carton as a glove and a stuffed sock for a ball and a branch for a bat.*
Sammy Tries Out for a Baseball Team: *When Sammy was sixteen he went to a team tryout and made it but he got switched to the white sox and then to cubs.*
Sammy Begins to Hit Home Runs: *He began hitting home runs on the cubs team.*
The Great Home Run Race: *In 1998 he hit sixty home runs then a total of sixty-six.*
A Hero on and off the Field: *Then he gave some money to the people so they could rebuild homes in his home country.*

Advanced Descriptor:

All important language/vocabulary from the text; good understanding of key words/concepts

Student Response Example:

Sammy as a Boy: *Sammy dreamed of playing baseball. He had to play baseball with a ball of socks for the ball a tree branch for the bat and a milk carton for the glove.*
Sammy Tries out for a Baseball Team: *When Sammy was 16 he went to the Rangers team to tryout. This was his chance to play in the United States. It was his dream and he made it.*
Sammy Begins to Hit Home Runs: *Playing in the United States was not easy. He spoke Spanish and very little English. He began to hit home runs.*
The Great Home Run Race: *Lots of baseball players were known for hitting home runs. Sammy was in a race with Mark McGuire to hit more than 61 home runs.*

		Mark won but Sammy hit 66 home runs. A Hero on and off the Field: The 1998 season was exciting for Sammy. He won many awards for his skills and for the good work he did for people in his country.
LITERAL COMPREHENSION **Prompt:** List 3 things that Sammy used to play baseball when he was a young boy.	**Independent Descriptor:** Accurate response **Student Response Example:** *1. a milk carton* *2. a stick* *3. a ball of socks*	**Advanced Descriptor:** Accurate response with specific details **Student Response Example:** *1. milk carton as a glove* *2. stuffed socks as a ball* *3. tree branch as a bat*
INTERPRETATION **Prompt:** Why do you think Sammy wants to help the people in his home country?	**Independent Descriptor:** Understands important text implications; may include supporting details **Student Response Example:** *Because he remembered he had a hard time when he was a kid.*	**Advanced Descriptor:** Insightful understanding of important text implications with supporting details **Student Response Example:** *I think he wants to help people in his home country because he has enough money to help them and he wants to be nice to his family and friends.*
REFLECTION **Prompt:** 1. What do you think is the most important thing that you learned from this book? 2. Tell why you think it is important.	**Independent Descriptor:** Significant message <u>and</u> a relevant reason for opinion **Student Response Example:** *1. That it's nice to be a hero when you're playing baseball, and when you're helping out other people.* *2. You're doing something for your team and other people.*	**Advanced Descriptor:** Significant message <u>and</u> reason for opinion that reflects higher-level thinking **Student Response Example:** *1. That Sammy Sosa was a great baseball player and did really good things for his country. He bought computers for schools and lots more good stuff.* *2. Because his country probably didn't have enough money to pay for all of that but he did.*

Student Written Responses

USE OF TEXT FEATURES

Prompt:
Think about the title, the pictures you have seen, and what you have read so far. Tell me what you know about Rosa and Hector.

Independent Descriptor:
Description of each character; includes at least 2 specific details
Student Response Example:
Rosa: *Rosa and Hector are at their grandmas and grandpas house and they are not having fun.*
Hector: *Hector likes video and computer games.*

Advanced Descriptor:
Description of each character; includes at least 3 specific details
Student Response Example:
Rosa: *Rosa is Hector's sister. They are used to having electronics but when they are at their grandma and grandpa's house they don't have any.*
Hector: *Hector thinks it is going to be boring.*

PREDICTION

Prompt:
What are 3 things you think might happen in the rest of this story?

Independent Descriptor:
At least 2 reasonable predictions that go beyond the text read aloud
Student Response Example:
1. *Rosa and Hector might go on a sled.*
2. *It goes through time.*
3. *They end up having a fun trip.*

Advanced Descriptor:
3 thoughtful predictions that go beyond the text read aloud
Student Response Example:
1. *I think they find something that has powers to travel through time.*
2. *They get a little freaked out and not scared but like a feeling you get when you're on an adventure.*
3. *Then they are having a lot of fun at the end.*

SCAFFOLDED SUMMARY

Independent Descriptor:
Summary in own language; includes important characters, many of the important events, and some details from the beginning, middle, and end

Advanced Descriptor:
Summary in own language; includes all important characters, events, and details from the beginning, middle, and end

SCAFFOLDED SUMMARY: VOCABULARY

Prompt:
Write a summary of this story in your own words. Include the important characters, events, and details. You may use the book and the words below to help you write your summary.

In the beginning,
Next,
Then,
After that,
In the end,

Independent Descriptor:
Most language/vocabulary from the text; basic understanding of most key words/concepts
Student Response Example:
In the beginning: *Rosa and Hector were asking their grandparents if they have a TV, DVD player, and more.*
Next: *Their grandparents said that they didn't need any so they didn't have any.*
Then: *Rosa and Hector said they will go outside and explore.*
After that: *They found a sled and traveled to the pilgrims in the 1620's. Then they went to another place.*
In the end: *They finally got back to their own time. They thought they would have a good time.*

Advanced Descriptor:
All important language/vocabulary from the text; good understanding of key words/concepts
Student Response Example:
In the beginning: *Hector and Rosa are going to their grandparents house. They think it will boring because they don't have a TV or computer.*
Next: *They go into the shed and find lots of old things. A sled takes them back in time to 1620 with the Pilgrims.*
Then: *They go to a different time and see a play about soldiers saving a queen and princess from a dragon.*
After that: *They want to go home again in 2006 in Vermont. They cross their fingers and their toes.*
In the end: *Rosa and Hector get back to their grandparents house. They think it will be the most exciting two weeks.*

LITERAL COMPREHENSION	Independent Descriptor:	Advanced Descriptor:
Prompt: List 3 things Rosa and Hector saw in the shed when they returned to their own time.	Accurate response **Student Response Example:** *1. clothes* *2. newspapers* *3. a doll*	Accurate response with specific details **Student Response Example:** *1. old hoop* *2. brown trunk* *3. rag doll*
INTERPRETATION	Independent Descriptor:	Advanced Descriptor:
Prompt: At the end of the story, why do you think Rosa and Hector thought it was going to be the most fun two weeks?	Understands important text implications; may include supporting details **Student Response Example:** *I think that they think there will be more adventures.*	Insightful understanding of important text implications; important supporting details **Student Response Example:** *Because they will play with the sled all 2 weeks and keep going back in time.*
REFLECTION	Independent Descriptor:	Advanced Descriptor:
Prompt: 1. What do you think is the most important event in the story? 2. Tell why you think it is important.	Significant event <u>and</u> a relevant reason for opinion **Student Response Example:** *1. When they pulled the lever on the sled.* *2. Because they got to travel through time.*	Significant event <u>and</u> reason(s) for opinion that reflects higher-level thinking **Student Response Example:** *1. That the grandparents had no TV.* *2. Because if they did Rosa and Hector wouldn't see the shed or find anything cool.*

Student Written Responses

Student Written Responses

USE OF TEXT FEATURES **Prompt:** Think about the title, the pictures you have seen, and what you have read so far. Tell me what you know about the mother beaver and her kits.	**Independent Descriptor:** Description of each character; includes at least 2 specific details **Student Response Example:** Mother Beaver: *The mother beaver is working on the dam. She is watching her babies.* Kits: *The kits are play fighting. They are on land.*	**Advanced Descriptor:** Description of each character; includes at least 3 specific details **Student Response Example:** Mother Beaver: *The mother beaver used her big tail and strong front paws to work on the dam. She liked her kits to stay close.* Kits: *The brother and sister kits played on the land. They move more quickly in water.*
PREDICTION **Prompt:** What are 3 things you think might happen in the rest of this story?	**Independent Descriptor:** At least 2 reasonable predictions that go beyond the text read aloud **Student Response Example:** 1. *Kits might get in danger.* 2. *Their mother and father might go looking for them.*	**Advanced Descriptor:** 3 thoughtful predictions that go beyond the text read aloud **Student Response Example:** 1. *The kits are going to get in trouble because a black bear is going to chase them.* 2. *The kits will go under water into the safe lodge.* 3. *The mother follows the kits in the lodge to keep them safe.*
SCAFFOLDED SUMMARY	**Independent Descriptor:** Summary in own language; includes important characters, many of the important events, and some details from the beginning, middle, and end	**Advanced Descriptor:** Summary in own language; includes all important characters, events, and details from the beginning, middle, and end
SCAFFOLDED SUMMARY: VOCABULARY **Prompt:** Write a summary of this story in your own words. Include the important characters, events, and details. You may use the book and the words below to help you write your summary. In the beginning, Next, Then, After that, In the end,	**Independent Descriptor:** Most language/vocabulary from the text; basic understanding of most key words/concepts **Student Response Example:** In the beginning: *Mother was working on the log dam watching her kits.* Next: *The kits were play wrestling and getting farther and farther from the water.* Then: *The mother saw a bear and tried to bring the bear down stream away from the kits.* After that: *The bear saw her and jumped in but the water was not deep so the beaver swam in till the water got deep and the bear went home.* In the end: *The mother went to the kits they were safe.*	**Advanced Descriptor:** All important language/vocabulary from the text; good understanding of key words/concepts **Student Response Example:** In the beginning: *There was a mother beaver that had two kits playing while she worked on the dam.* Next: *While the kits were playing they wandered farther away. A black bear appeared. The mother got the bears attention so he wouldnt see the kits.* Then: *The bear chased after the mother beaver. It was a long chase. The mother almost got caught a few times.* After that: *The bear gave up. Then it was safe for the kits to come back to the dam.* In the end: *Finally everyone was safe. The kits couldnt go more than a few feet from the water.*

Student Written Responses

LITERAL COMPREHENSION	**Independent Descriptor:** Accurate response **Student Response Example:** *1. old* *2. black* *3. hungry*	**Advanced Descriptor:** Accurate response with specific details **Student Response Example:** *1. old black bear* *2. weak old eyes* *3. hungry and smelling the air*
Prompt: List 3 ways the bear was described.		
INTERPRETATION	**Independent Descriptor:** Understands important text implications; may include supporting details **Student Response Example:** *Because another bear might come and the kits could get hurt.*	**Advanced Descriptor:** Insightful understanding of important text implications with supporting details or rationale **Student Response Example:** *Because she didn't want anything to happen like what happened with the bear.*
Prompt: At the end of the story, why wouldn't the mother beaver let the kits go more than a few feet from the water?		
REFLECTION	**Independent Descriptor:** Significant event <u>and</u> a relevant reason for opinion **Student Response Example:** *1. The mom got home safe.* *2. So she could take care of her babies.*	**Advanced Descriptor:** Significant event <u>and</u> reason for opinion that reflects higher-level thinking **Student Response Example:** *1. When the mom got the bears attention.* *2. She didn't want her kits to die and she saved their lives by getting the bears attention.*
Prompt: 1. What do you think is the most important event in this story? 2. Tell why you think it is important.		

Student Written Responses

Level 40 F *All the Way Under*

QUESTIONING/ PREDICTION	Independent Descriptor:	Advanced Descriptor:
Prompt: List 3 questions that you had while reading the first part of this story.	At least 2 reasonable questions and predictions that go beyond the text read aloud **Student Response Example:** *1. Why can't she go in the water, you don't have to swim?* *2. Why didn't she tell the truth?*	At least 3 thoughtful questions and predictions that go beyond the text read aloud **Student Response Example:** *1. What will happen when Sonya goes in the ocean?* *2. Will Sonya confess and say she can't swim?* *3. Will Sonya go under the water?*
What are 3 things that you think might happen in the rest of this story?	*1. That it won't be so bad to go in the water.* *2. Maybe she will get embarrassed in front of her cousin.*	*1. I think Sonya will try to hold off going in the ocean.* *2. I think if Sonya goes in the ocean she won't go in far.* *3. I also think Sonya will conquer her fear of going down under the water.*
SUMMARY	**Independent Descriptor:**	**Advanced Descriptor:**
Prompt: Write a summary of this story in your own words. Include the important characters, events, and details from the beginning, middle, and end of the story. You may use the book to help you write your summary.	Summary in own language; includes most of the important characters' names, some details, and many of the important events in sequence from the beginning, middle, and end **Student Response Example:** *Sonya came to the beach with Katie. Katie raced to the ocean. Sonya didn't know how to swim, so she took her time doing things. But when Katie said are you afraid of the water No Sonya said. So she went in the water. There was a big wave and something got her leg. She cried for the life guard. When the life guard picked it up it was sea weed. So they got ice cream. Then the life guard taught Sonya how to go in the water. After that she had fun.*	Well-organized summary in own language; includes all important characters' names, specific details, and all important events from the beginning, middle, and end **Student Response Example:** *In the beginning of the story Sonya, Katie, Uncle Jack, and Aunt Lisa went to the beach. When they got there Katie jumped right in the ocean. Sonya, Katie's cousin, tried to hold off going into the water because she was afraid.* *In the middle Katie asked Sonya if she was afraid of the water and Sonya said no. So Sonya and Katie were going into the water. Katie was pulling Sonya to a big wave and Sonya tried to run away from it but she got hit by it. When she got up she felt like a octopus was pulling her down under the water. She yelled for help and the lifeguard came to her and rescued her. Sonya felt embarrassed that it was a piece of seaweed.* *At the end Uncle Jack got Katie and Sonya ice cream. The lifeguard and Katie taught Sonya to go all the way under. And they had fun.*

LITERAL COMPREHENSION	**Independent Descriptor:** Information from the text that accurately responds to question(s) or prompt(s)	**Advanced Descriptor:** All important information from the text that effectively responds to question(s) or prompt(s)
Prompt: List 3 things that you know about Sonya.	**Student Response Example:** 1. She was afraid of the water. 2. She learns to be in the water. 3. She has fun.	**Student Response Example:** 1. She can not swim. 2. She is afraid to go under the water. 3. She does not want anyone to know.
INTERPRETATION	**Independent Descriptor:** Understands important text implications; relevant supporting details	**Advanced Descriptor:** Insightful understanding of important text implications; important supporting details
Prompt: How did Sonya's feeling about being at the beach change in this story?	**Student Response Example:** She was happy at the end because she learned to dunk her head under.	**Student Response Example:** Sonya was afraid at first. Sonya's feeling changes because when she got to know how to dunk her head under water and surf the waves and when she knew that a lifeguard was there in case anything happened in the water she liked it.
REFLECTION	**Independent Descriptor:** Significant message or event <u>and</u> a relevant reason for opinion	**Advanced Descriptor:** Significant message or event <u>and</u> reason(s) for opinion that reflects higher-level thinking
Prompt: 1. What do you think is the most important event in this story? 2. Tell why you think that event is important.	**Student Response Example:** 1. When the lifeguard tells her she will teach her how to swim. 2. Because then she learns not to be afraid and can go in the water.	**Student Response Example:** 1. The most important event is when Sonya fought her fears and went into the water. 2. It is important because if she didn't go in the water she would of stayed afraid.
METACOGNITIVE AWARENESS	**Independent Descriptor:** At least 1 specific example from the text related to the identified strategy; may include details	**Advanced Descriptor:** At least 2 specific examples from the text related to the identified strategy; includes details
Prompt: Check 1 strategy that you used to help you understand this story. Give at least 2 specific examples from this story that show how you used this comprehension strategy.	**Student Response Example:** I pictured what was happening. On page four and five I pictured them in my head at the beach.	**Student Response Example:** I asked myself questions as I read. In the part when Sonya was drowning I asked myself if she was going to make it back alive. Then I asked if she would learn how to swim.

Student Written Responses

Level 40 NF *The Amazing Octopus*

QUESTIONING/ PREDICTION	Independent Descriptor:	Advanced Descriptor:
Prompt: What questions did you have as you were reading the first part of this text? What do you think you will learn from reading the rest of this text?	At least 2 reasonable questions and predictions that go beyond the text read aloud **Student Response Example:** 1. What does cold-blooded mean? 2. How does it use gills and funnels to breathe? 1. How long the life is. 2. How they have amazing abilities. 3. How does the life cycle look like?	At least 3 thoughtful questions and predictions that go beyond the text read aloud **Student Response Example:** 1. Why does an octopus live in the ocean? 2. How big can the octopus get? 3. Why does it have a big head? 1. How an octopus survives. 2. Where it gets its food. 3. The life cycle of an octopus.
SUMMARY **Prompt:** Write a summary of this book in your own words. Include the important ideas and facts from each section. You may use the book to help you write your summary.	**Independent Descriptor:** Summary in own language; includes many important ideas, some vocabulary, and supporting facts from each section **Student Response Example:** *The octopus is a cold-blooded creature. More than 150 kinds can be found in the world. The biggest octopus is 20 feet from arm tip to arm tip. The octopus eats meat, sees well in the dark, and hunts alone. When the meals come, the octopus floats down like an open flower and traps it. Then they squirt poison in it. After that the prey dies quickly. If the octopus is alarmed, it changes it's color for protection. They like to hide. They use tricks to survive. To scare predators, the octopus puffs up and flashes fake "eyes." Octopuses live alone, most of their lives. When the mom makes the den, she lays 100,000 eggs. Only a few babies live.*	**Advanced Descriptor:** Summary in own language; includes all important ideas, key vocabulary, and supporting facts from each section **Student Response Example:** *Octopus live deep in the ocean. A octopus has 8 arms and on the arms are suckers. Many kinds of octopuses have 2,000 suckers. A octopus has 2 eyes that can turn a half circle. A octopus eats meat. Every night a octopus glides on the ocean floor with its suckers looking for food. Octopuses make a web of themselves when prey comes it closes down. When a octopus gets alarmed it changes color. When a eel comes to a octopus and the octopus can't escape it leaves arm behind. Octopuses live in caves. Males die soon after mating. A female octopus lays 100,000 eggs and cleans them with their suckers. Only a small number of the eggs survive. Octopuses have amazing abilities like they can change color and blend in with the environment.*

LITERAL COMPREHENSION	**Independent Descriptor:**	**Advanced Descriptor:**
Prompt: List 3 facts about an octopus.	Information from the text that accurately responds to question(s) or prompt(s) **Student Response Example:** 1. *They can turn their eyes in half circles* 2. *They use their suckers to clean their babies* 3. *Their skin can change colors*	All important information from the text that effectively responds to question(s) or prompt(s) **Student Response Example:** 1. *Octopuses have two eyes that can turn in half circles without moving their heads.* 2. *Octopuses have suckers they use to pick up food, to crawl, and to cling to things.* 3. *Octopuses have skin that can change colors and patterns to help them hide and to catch prey.*
INTERPRETATION **Prompt:** What do you think would happen if there were no octopus predators in the ocean?	**Independent Descriptor:** Understands important text implication(s); relevant supporting details **Student Response Example:** 1. *Octopuses would survive in the ocean.* 2. *Since they lay 100,000 eggs there would be too many.*	**Advanced Descriptor:** Insightful understanding of important text implications; important supporting details **Student Response Example:** 1. *There would be more baby octopuses that live and grow into adults.* 2. *There would be less tiny prey that young octopuses eat because there are more octopuses.* 3. *More octopuses will mate as adults.*
REFLECTION **Prompt:** 1. What do you think is the most important thing about octopuses? 2. Tell why you think this is important.	**Independent Descriptor:** Significant message or information <u>and</u> a relevant reason for opinion **Student Response Example:** 1. *That they would use tricks to survive.* 2. *Well they want to live so they use their tricks like shooting water to stop them trying to eat them.*	**Advanced Descriptor:** Significant message or information <u>and</u> reason(s) for opinion that reflects higher-level thinking **Student Response Example:** 1. *I think camouflage is one of the most important.* 2. *Camouflage is one of the abilities that help them survive the predators.*
METACOGNITIVE AWARENESS **Prompt:** Check 1 strategy that you used to help you understand this text. Give at least 2 specific examples from this book that show how you used this comprehension strategy.	**Independent Descriptor:** At least 1 specific example from the text related to the identified strategy; may include details **Student Response Example:** *I pictured what was happening when something cool was described and it had no pictures, like breaking off a leg.*	**Advanced Descriptor:** At least 2 specific examples from the text related to the identified strategy; includes details **Student Response Example:** *I asked myself questions as I read. I asked why do female octopuses shoot the babies out of the den and then die and why do only so few babies live.*

Student Written Responses

Level 40 F *A Journey to Freedom*

QUESTIONING/ PREDICTION

Prompt:
List 3 questions that you had while reading the first part of this story.

What are 3 things that you think might happen in the rest of this story?

Independent Descriptor:
At least 2 reasonable questions and predictions that go beyond the text read aloud
Student Response Example:
1. Do they have food to eat?
2. Where are they going?

1. I think they might go to the north.
2. Maybe someone caught them.
3. They are going to be happy if they reach freedom.

Advanced Descriptor:
At least 3 thoughtful questions and predictions that go beyond the text read aloud
Student Response Example:
1. Where will they go after they run away?
2. Does anyone help them along the way?
3. How did Bess know which way to go?

1. Jed and Bess will go through and get to freedom.
2. They will use the underground railroad.
3. They will help other people.

SUMMARY

Prompt:
Write a summary of this story in your own words. Include the important characters, events, and details from the beginning, middle, and end of the story. You may use the book to help you write your summary.

Independent Descriptor:
Summary in own language; includes most of the important characters' names, some details, and many of the important events in sequence from the beginning, middle, and end
Student Response Example:
The main characters are Jed and Bess. One night they were in the cabin and his mother told him we have to leave because Master Boyd's son is going to try to sell young slaves. Jed's mother did not want them to be separated. So Jed got his things and they were off. Bess looked in the sky for a signal and said to Jed if anything happens follow the North Star that I showed you every night of your life. The following night they saw a light in the house. That meant it was safe. They knocked on the door and a man and woman helped them. They gave them food and clothes. The next day another person came to help them go to the next safe house. The next day Bess came up with a fever. Jed and the Scotts cared for her until she was well. The ferryman came to help to cross the river. They were free.

Advanced Descriptor:
Well-organized summary in own language; includes all important characters' names, specific details, and all important events from the beginning, middle, and end
Student Response Example:
Bess and Jed were running away because they were slaves. They headed for the underground railroad. The first stop was at a white man and woman's house. They could tell it was safe because it had a lantern on the post and a quilt on the line. A man knocked on the door and said I am a friend of a friend so they knew he was safe. Then the man put Bess and Jed in the false bottom of a wagon. When they got to the next house it had lots of strong smells. They showed Bess and Jed a secret room for them to sleep in. When they woke up the woman told Bess and Jed that they made all those strong scents to throw the dogs off track of their scent. Then another man took them on a long journey. Then he handed them ferry tickets. The ferry man was a friend of a friend too. The ferry man took them across. Then they were free. A woman named Rose met them in the north. They were safe and they could make their own decisions.

LITERAL COMPREHENSION **Prompt:** List 3 things that you know about Jed.	**Independent Descriptor:** Information from the text that accurately responds to question(s) or prompt(s) **Student Response Example:** *1. Jed worries a little.* *2. He wants to be a conductor.* *3. He is free, no more a slave.*	**Advanced Descriptor:** All important information from the text that effectively responds to question(s) or prompt(s) **Student Response Example:** *1. At first Jed is worried.* *2. Jed is young so he doesn't know about the Underground Railroad.* *3. Jed wants to be a conductor some day.*
INTERPRETATION **Prompt:** Why do you think Jed wanted to be an Underground Railroad conductor?	**Independent Descriptor:** Understands important text implication(s); relevant supporting details **Student Response Example:** *I think Jed wants to be an underground railroad conductor because he wants to help other slaves escape.*	**Advanced Descriptor:** Insightful understanding of important text implications; important supporting details **Student Response Example:** *I think Jed would join the underground railroad because he wants to help other slaves escape and be free like him and see the people be happy.*
REFLECTION **Prompt:** 1. What do you think is the most important event in this story? 2. Tell why you think that event is important.	**Independent Descriptor:** Significant message or event <u>and</u> a relevant reason for opinion. **Student Response Example:** *1. Them running away.* *2. Because Jed won't be separated from Bess.*	**Advanced Descriptor:** Significant message or event <u>and</u> reason(s) for opinion that reflects higher-level thinking. **Student Response Example:** *1. I think that the most important event is when Jed and his mother are free from slavery.* *2. It took courage for them to be free. Slaves shall have the right to be free and not told what to do.*
METACOGNITIVE AWARENESS **Prompt:** Check 1 strategy that you used to help you understand this story. Give at least 2 specific examples from this story that show how you used this comprehension strategy.	**Independent Descriptor:** At least 1 specific example from the text related to the identified strategy; may include details **Student Response Example:** *I pictured what was happening.* *Like when they got in the cabinet I pictured two people getting in a cabinet.*	**Advanced Descriptor:** At least 2 specific examples from the text related to the identified strategy; includes details **Student Response Example:** *I asked myself questions as I read.* *I asked myself if Jed and Bess were actually going to run away and be safe. And I asked myself if they would get caught in the woods.*

Student Written Responses

117

QUESTIONING/ PREDICTION	Independent Descriptor:	Advanced Descriptor:
Prompt: What questions did you have as you were reading the first part of this text? What do you think you will learn from reading the rest of this text?	At least 2 reasonable questions and predictions that go beyond the text read aloud **Student Response Example:** *1. Why are their eyes yellow?* *2. How do they hunt?* *1. How they hunt their meals.* *2. Why their ears are pointed.* *3. Why they howl.*	At least 3 thoughtful questions and predictions that go beyond the text read aloud **Student Response Example:** *1. Where is the most common place wolves settle?* *2. Which type of wolves are most found?* *3. Why do wolves howl?* *1. I would learn how and what they do to get their food.* *2. I would learn how many wolves are in a pack.* *3. What it means when wolves howl.*
SUMMARY	Independent Descriptor:	Advanced Descriptor:
Prompt: Write a summary of this book in your own words. Include the important ideas and facts from each section. You may use the book to help you write your summary.	Summary in own language; includes many important ideas, some vocabulary, and supporting facts from each section **Student Response Example:** *There are five different types of gray wolves. There is Arctic wolf, Eastern Timber wolf, Great Plains wolf, Mexican wolf, and Rocky Mountain wolf. Gray wolves live in packs about 6 to 15. Gray wolves are also known for their howl. Their howl warns others to stay away. Gray wolves hunt large animals like deer or elk. Some wolves go for the throat while other wolves grab the hind legs. Female wolves give birth from 4 to 6 pups. After 6 months the pups are old enough to hunt their prey. People who value wolves are trying to save them.*	Summary in own language; includes all important ideas, key vocabulary, and supporting facts from each section **Student Response Example:** *This is about wolves. Wolves travel in a pack. In a pack are 6 to 15 wolves. There are 5 types of wolves:* *1. Rocky Mountain wolf* *2. Mexican wolf* *3. Great Plains wolf* *4. Eastern timber wolf* *5. Arctic wolf* *Wolves howl for 5 reasons. They howl to keep the wolf pack together, warn other packs to keep out, start a chase, and for fun.* *Wolves work together to hunt. While one wolf bites the elk's rear leg another one bites its neck. Each wolf eats 20 pounds of meat. Each wolf has a rank. The rank tells when it is your turn to eat.* *The leader leads the hunt, divides the food, and settles fights. The leader is the only one that mates and has pups.* *There are people today who are working to find ways to protect wolves and where they live.*

Student Written Responses

LITERAL COMPREHENSION	Independent Descriptor:	Advanced Descriptor:
Prompt: List 3 facts about gray wolves.	Information from the text that accurately responds to question(s) or prompt(s) **Student Response Example:** *1. There are 5 types of wolves.* *2. They eat moose.* *3. The leader has pups.*	All important information from the text that effectively responds to question(s) or prompt(s) **Student Response Example:** *1. There are 5 types of gray wolves in North America.* *2. Adult gray wolves can weigh between 50 and 145 pounds.* *3. Their fur can range in color from white to gray to black.*
INTERPRETATION **Prompt:** Why do you think wolves are able to survive in the wild?	Independent Descriptor: Understands important text implication(s); relevant supporting details **Student Response Example:** *I think they are able to survive in the wild because they live in big packs. They have good hunting skills and they can kill an animal twice their size.*	Advanced Descriptor: Insightful understanding of important text implications; important supporting details **Student Response Example:** *I think wolves can survive the wild because they are good hunters. They live in groups called packs. They work together to catch their prey. They all survive because they divide up the food.*
REFLECTION **Prompt:** 1. What do you think is the most important thing about gray wolves? 2. Tell why you think this is important.	Independent Descriptor: Significant message or information <u>and</u> a relevant reason for opinion **Student Response Example:** *1. That they kill a really big prey.* *2. So that they have enough meat for everyone.*	Advanced Descriptor: Significant message or information <u>and</u> reason(s) for opinion that reflects higher-level thinking **Student Response Example:** *1. That gray wolves are about to be extinct.* *2. They need to be protected and if they aren't they will be all dead. Having laws to protect them is important.*
METACOGNITIVE AWARENESS **Prompt:** Check 1 strategy that you used to help you understand this text. Give at least 2 specific examples from this book that show how you used this comprehension strategy.	Independent Descriptor: At least 1 specific example from the text related to the identified strategy; may include details **Student Response Example:** *I pictured when people started to kill the wolves and killed 9 of 10.*	Advanced Descriptor: At least 2 specific examples from the text related to the identified strategy; includes details **Student Response Example:** *I pictured what was happening. When they were catching the prey I would picture it in my head how they were doing it. I also pictured wolves howling in a pack.*

Student Written Responses

Moving Into Instruction

As stated in the introduction, *DRA2, K–3*, is designed for kindergarten through third-grade classrooms with rich literate environments. A wide variety of developmentally appropriate books and other reading materials are available and accessible for students to read, reread, and enjoy. Reading and writing are taught as reciprocal processes and the planned activities, experiences, and assignments for the language arts block of time are meaningful to students. On a daily basis, all students

- **hear a variety of literature read aloud**
- **read independently for a sustained period of time**
- **respond to literature in a variety of ways**
- **receive instruction, support, and specific feedback in guided reading/writing groups, individual conferences, and/or in mini-lessons**

Developmentally appropriate assessments, such as *DRA2, K–3*, are truly an integral part of the teaching-learning process. They cannot stand alone. What happens before and after the assessment is most important. Information obtained from the assessment benefits both students and teachers only when it is used to guide instruction. The areas you check on the Focus for Instruction: Class Profile for each of the four stages of learning to read (Emergent, Early, Transitional, and Extending) identify what students need to learn next. Knowing this information will help you make more effective teaching decisions.

When choosing the most effective instructional techniques, it is important to value the reciprocity of the reading and writing processes. What students read has a definite impact on what they write. Writing personal narratives, informational pieces, and stories helps with comprehension. As developing readers learn how to analyze and work with words, they use what they know about letter/sound relationships, spelling patterns, and meaning units to decode words while reading and to spell words while writing.

This section, Moving Into Instruction, is designed to assist you in thinking about and planning for instruction that is based on your students' needs within the four stages of learning to read. It includes an overview in chart form of what Emergent, Early, Transitional, and Extending readers generally are able to do (control) and what they are in the process of learning. Common characteristics of the texts at the various stages as well as the strategic reading behaviors students need to learn are also shown in chart form as a reference.

On pages 130–139, there are generic blackline masters you may use in your classroom instruction. Select which masters you feel are most appropriate for first, second, or third grade.

Overview of Reading Stages: Emergent

In the Emergent stage of learning to read, shared and interactive writing are an effective means of modeling and teaching students how to attend to printed language, concepts of print, and letter-sound relationships. It is important to read aloud engaging books and simple poetry every day, as well as sing simple songs and nursery rhymes that students enjoy. These activities foster not only a love for reading but also the development of students' awareness of and the ability to attend to words and sounds in words.

Alphabet activities and picture sorts involving beginning letter sounds provide a means for students to build their knowledge of letter-sound relationships.

Emerging readers/writers benefit from having many opportunities to write. Through writing, these students are learning to use their knowledge about letters, sounds, and words to construct simple messages. Giving them specific feedback as they read aloud what they have written reinforces what they control and provides direction for what they need to learn next.

As Emerging readers develop early strategies of left-to-right and one-to-one matching, they also benefit from shared reading experiences.

The following three charts will give you an overview of what Emerging readers generally control and are learning to do, the type of texts they read, and what you are to draw their attention to and teach before, during, and after reading a book.

Emergent Readers (*DRA*2 Levels A–3; Guided Reading Levels A–B)		
	Generally are able to . . .	**Are learning to . . .**
Reading Engagement	• hold a book and turn the pages. • look at the illustrations/photographs in books. • identify and talk about a favorite story or book.	• select familiar texts for independent reading. • read familiar patterned texts independently for a short period of time. • talk about a favorite part of the book or story.
Oral Reading Fluency	• recall a modeled simple sentence pattern. • move left to right on at least one line of text.	• consistently match one-to-one (spoken word with written word). • recognize a few high-frequency words (e.g., *the, I, in, he*). • monitor using known words and text-picture match. • identify letter/sound relationships. • use beginning letter/sound relationships to problem-solve words. • use beginning letter/sound relationships to confirm or discount word choice.
Comprehension	• identify or name familiar objects and/or actions depicted in illustrations/photographs.	• understand the words used to talk about printed language concepts (e.g., *word, letter, begin, end, first, last, sound,* and so on). • talk about what is happening in the illustrations or photographs. • recall some events in a story. • talk about favorite part of the book or story.

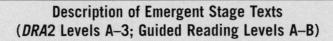

Description of Emergent Stage Texts
(*DRA*2 Levels A–3; Guided Reading Levels A–B)

Content
- familiar objects, actions, situations
- familiar vocabulary
- illustrations and photographs provide a high level of support

Genre/Text Structure
- simple recount
- caption book
- simple narrative

Language/Word Structures
- oral language structures
- very simple written language structures
- 1 to 3 sentence patterns with 1 to 2 word changes
- common high-frequency words and other predictable words

Layout
- consistent placement of text
- 1 to 3 lines of text
- up to 50 words
- larger font size with large spaces between words and lines of text

---

Emergent Strategic Reading Behaviors

Scaffold (Model, Teach, and Reinforce) Emergent Readers to . . .

Before Reading	• look at the cover illustration and think about the text. • listen to the book introduction given by the teacher. • look at the cover illustrations or photographs and tell what is pictured or what is happening. • listen and watch as the teacher models reading one or more pages.
During Reading	• use prior knowledge of the content, the pictures, and the modeled-sentence pattern to read the text. • problem-solve unknown words using pictures and prior knowledge, sentence structure, and initial letter/sound relationships. • monitor using one-to-one match, picture-text match, and known words. • cross-check when a word does not make sense, sound right, and/or look right. • self-correct miscues that do not make sense, sound right, and/or look right.
After Reading	• identify a part of the book they liked best and tell why.

Moving Into Instruction

122

In the Early stage, shared and interactive writing are effective means of teaching students how words, sentences, and stories are constructed. Shared/interactive experiences help Early readers learn how to

- attend to printed language
- segment words into onset and rime or phonemes
- identify sound(s) and write the corresponding letter(s)
- reread to monitor what they have written so far and plan what to write next

It is critical that teachers scaffold the selection of texts so that these readers are daily reading books that are at the appropriate level of challenge. Identifying a range of leveled texts from which students may choose will enable them to select "just right" texts for independent reading. It is also important for Early readers to have time to read and enjoy different genres on a daily basis.

Independent reading time needs to be closely monitored to see that these Early readers are actually reading. Having students take turns reading to and listening to a partner after they have read independently will increase the amount of time and the number of texts they read.

Early readers need to develop a growing core of known words that they can read quickly. These words provide a basis for decoding less familiar words. Providing students with timely and specific feedback about their writing and spelling helps them become better writers and attend more closely to word and/or letter features. Word-sorting activities also help these Early readers to attend to letter sequences within words.

The following three charts will give you an overview of what Early readers generally control and are learning to do, the type of texts they read, and what you are to draw their attention to and teach before, during, and after reading a book.

Early Readers (*DRA*2 Levels 4–12; Guided Reading Levels C–G)		
	Generally are able to . . .	**Are learning to . . .**
Reading Engagement	• select familiar texts for independent reading. • read familiar patterned texts independently for a short period of time. • tell about a favorite book.	• select new texts from a range of leveled sets for independent reading. • sustain independent reading for a longer period of time.
Oral Reading Fluency	• consistently match one-to-one. • quickly recognize high-frequency words (e.g., *the, I, in, he*). • monitor using known words and text-picture match. • quickly identify familiar letter/sound relationships. • use beginning letter/sound relationships to problem-solve words. • use beginning letter(s)/sound(s) to confirm or discount word choice.	• scan pages from top to bottom to locate text. • hold the story line while accessing visual information. • use meaning, structure, and visual information to problem-solve unknown words. • use dominant letter(s)/sound(s) to confirm or discount word choice. • decode one-syllable words by sequentially blending letter sounds. • use familiar letter sequences (onsets and rimes) to decode unknown words. • use analogies to decode words with similar spelling patterns (e.g., *day, night*). • read in 2–3-word phrases. • read dialogue with expression.
Comprehension	• understand the words used to talk about printed language concepts (*word, letter, begin, end, first, last, sound*, and so on). • talk about what is happening in the illustrations or photographs. • recall some events in a story. • talk about a favorite part of the book or story.	• preview a text; construct tentative meaning using the illustrations or photographs. • orally retell the story or information. • identify a favorite part of a story and tell why. • make text-to-self connections.

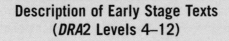

Description of Early Stage Texts
(*DRA2* Levels 4–12)

Content
- familiar objects, actions, situations
- familiar vocabulary
- illustrations and photographs provide a high level of support

Genre/Text Structure
- realistic narratives with a sequence of events
- simple fairy tales and folktales
- simple informational texts
- simple poetry and songs

Language/Word Structures
- blend of oral and written language structures
- varied sentences with repeated phrases or refrains
- common high-frequency words, decodable 1–2 syllable words, fairly predictable words

Layout
- varied placement of text
- print placement support phrasing
- approximately 2–6 lines of text (50 to 150 words)

Early Strategic Reading Behaviors

Scaffold (Model, Teach, and Reinforce) Early Readers to . . .

Before Reading	• look at the cover illustration and think about the text (*What is this about? What kind of book is this? Where do I start reading?*). • listen to the book introduction given by the teacher. • look at the illustrations/photographs and tell what is happening.
During Reading	• use prior knowledge of the content, the pictures, and the printed text to read the book. • monitor using one-to-one match, picture-text match, and known words. • problem-solve unknown words using pictures, prior knowledge, sentence structure, and initial letter(s)/sound(s) relationships. • cross-check and self-correct when a word does not make sense, sound right, and/or look right. • monitor meaning; stop and reread when meaning is not clear. • predict what they think will happen next.
After Reading	• retell what they read with support/prompts. • identify a part of the book they liked best and tell why. • make text-to-self and text-to-text connections.

Transitional readers benefit from guided reading group experiences as well as buddy reading and independent reading times. Monitored independent reading provides students with opportunities to practice and reinforce new learning and should be a part of each school day.

Generally, Transitional readers are learning to read with increasing fluency. It is important to provide authentic reasons for rereading, such as reading aloud a favorite section of a book or poem to the class/group, participating in readers' theater, and audiotaping a portion of a text to self-assess his or her oral reading. Students may also do repeated readings of short passages in order to improve their reading rate and/or expression.

At this stage, students still need assistance selecting novel texts. Identifying a range of leveled texts from which students may select will ensure that they select "just right" material for independent reading. It is also important to encourage Transitional readers to read a variety of books and genres—narrative, informational, folktales, simple fantasies, poetry, etc.

Transitional readers/writers need timely and specific feedback about their independent writing (e.g., ideas, word choice, spelling, basic punctuation) to help them become better writers and readers, especially when their attention is focused on how other authors construct stories, informational pieces, etc. Calling their attention to their spelling helps them attend to letter sequences and patterns within words. Teacher-directed activities such as sorting words with long vowel patterns, segmenting polysyllabic words into syllables, and substituting beginning blends and inflectional endings also help these students to attend to words' letter sequences and vowel patterns. These types of activities increase students' awareness of how words are constructed and/or taken apart, a necessary skill for reading and writing.

The following three charts will give you an overview of what Transitional readers generally control and are learning to do, the type of texts they read, and what you are to draw their attention to and teach before, during, and after reading a book.

Transitional Readers (*DRA*2 Levels 14–24; Guided Reading Levels H–L)		
	Generally are able to . . .	**Are learning to . . .**
Reading Engagement	• select novel texts from leveled sets for independent reading. • sustain independent reading for a short period of time. • tell about a favorite book.	• select novel texts from a range of leveled sets for independent reading. • sustain independent reading for a longer period of time. • read several familiar and/or novel texts independently at one sitting. • read a beginning chapter book across several sittings. • read different genres (e.g., simple biographies, simple mysteries, poetry).
Oral Reading Fluency	• scan pages from top to bottom to locate text. • hold the story line while accessing visual information. • use meaning, structure, and visual information to problem-solve unknown words. • use dominant letter(s)/sound(s) to confirm or discount word choice. • decode one-syllable words by sequentially blending letter sounds. • use familiar letter sequences (onsets and rimes) to decode unknown words. • use analogies to decode words with similar spelling patterns (e.g., *day*, *may*). • read in 2–3 word phrases.	• use multiple cues to problem-solve words quickly. • take words apart (onsets, rimes, endings, contractions, compound words) to decode unknown words. • search and monitor vowel patterns within words. • use analogies to decode words with common spelling patterns (e.g., *out*, *shout*). • quickly self-correct significant miscues. • read in longer phrases. • attend to and read punctuation. • read dialogue with expression. • read at an appropriate rate.

Transitional Readers continued
(*DRA*2 Levels 14–24; Guided Reading Levels H–L)

	Generally are able to . . .	Are learning to . . .
Comprehension	<ul><li>preview a text; construct tentative meaning using the illustrations or photographs.</li><li>orally retell the story or information.</li><li>identify a favorite part of a story and tell why.</li><li>make text-to-self connections.</li></ul>	<ul><li>make predictions based on prior knowledge, the book title, and oral book introduction.</li><li>extract more meaning from the text; rely less on the illustrations.</li><li>monitor meaning across pages/short chapters.</li><li>recall main ideas and supporting details from previously read chapters or segments to continue constructing and monitoring meaning.</li><li>use fix-up strategies when meaning is not clear.</li><li>identify important ideas, details, and vocabulary to include in a retelling.</li><li>retell important ideas and details sequentially or in a logical order.</li><li>identify story elements (e.g., characters, setting, problem, solution).</li><li>make inferences and discuss what is implied or suggested in the text.</li><li>gain information from text features (e.g., book/chapter titles, headings, table of contents).</li><li>understand basic information presented graphically (e.g., simple maps, charts, timelines).</li><li>make text-to-text connections.</li><li>identify the most important event and tell why it is important.</li><li>support opinions with examples from the text or personal experience.</li></ul>

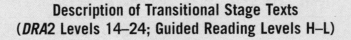

Description of Transitional Stage Texts
(*DRA*2 Levels 14–24; Guided Reading Levels H–L)

Content
- familiar and novel experiences, topics, and themes
- familiar as well as specialized and/or more challenging vocabulary
- illustrations and photographs provide a high level of support
- some information presented graphically in nonfiction texts
- characters are memorable

Genre/Text Structure
- variety of genres (realistic fiction, simple fantasies, basic informational texts, humor, poetry)
- traditional retellings of fairy tales/folktales
- repeated events and episodic chapters (beginning chapter books)
- series (e.g., *Henry and Mudge, Cam Jansen, Nate the Great, Frog and Toad*)

Language/Word Structures
- oral, written, and literary language structures
- large numbers of familiar/high-frequency words
- dialogue used to move the story along
- some descriptive language

Layout
- multiple lines of text per page
- may have some full pages of print (up to 20 lines of text)
- illustrations extend the text, depict characters and setting
- clear spacing between words and lines of text

Transitional Strategic Reading Behaviors	
Scaffold (Model, Teach, and Reinforce) Transitional Readers to . . .	
Before Reading	• look at the title and the cover illustration and think about the text (*What is this about? What kind of book is this? What are my expectations?*). • look at the illustrations/photographs and tell or think about what is happening. • preview texts, making predictions about what is likely to happen or identifying topics and information that may be included. • listen to the book introduction given by the teacher.
During Reading	• predict what they think will happen next; confirm and/or alter predictions. • read text with an appropriate rate, phrasing, and expression. • quickly problem-solve unknown/challenging words using multiple sources of information (e.g., meaning, sentence structure, visual). • take apart longer, unknown words (e.g., syllables, endings, common letter sequences) but also use letter-sounding if needed. • quickly self-correct significant miscues. • read silently. • monitor meaning across pages, segments, and/or chapters; stop and reread when meaning is not clear or lost.
After Reading	• include important characters, events, ideas, and details in oral retellings. • organize information presented in a retelling in a sequential or logical order. • identify a part of the book they liked best and tell why. • discuss text-to-self and text-to-text connections made while reading. • demonstrate understanding of the characters through discussion. • identify the most important thing that happened in the story. • use details from the text and personal experience to support opinion(s).

Overview of Reading Stages: Extending

It is important for readers in the Extending stage to read a variety of books, enjoy different genres, keep a record of what they have read, and write in response to their reading. At this stage, students generally read independently for longer periods of time and need less support, but they continue to benefit from guided reading group experiences, literature circles, and other book groups.

Generally, Extending readers are learning to read with more effective expression. It is still important to provide authentic reasons for rereading, such as participating in readers' theater and audiotaping a portion of a text to self-assess his or her oral reading. If needed, students may do repeated readings of short passages to improve their reading rate.

Asking students to read aloud their own writing with expression often enables them to hear the natural pauses and monitor their use of punctuation. As in the other stages of learning to read, Extending

readers/writers need timely and specific feedback about their independent writing (e.g., ideas, word choice, spelling, punctuation).

Extending readers will encounter more polysyllabic words as they read longer, more complex texts. It is important for these students to learn how to analyze words with two or more syllables, as well as identify meaning units within words (e.g., prefixes, base words, and/or suffixes) in guided reading and/or mini-lessons. Word sorts consisting of common syllable patterns, affixes, and/or base words help these developing readers attend to letter sequences, vowel patterns, and meaning units within words.

The following three charts will give you an overview of what Extending readers generally control and are learning to do, the type of texts they read, and what you are to draw their attention to and teach before, during, and after reading a book.

Extending Readers
(*DRA*2 Levels 28–38; Guided Reading Levels M–P)

	Generally are able to . . .	Are learning to . . .
Reading Engagement	• select novel texts from a range of leveled sets for independent reading. • sustain independent reading for a longer period of time. • read several familiar and/or novel texts independently at one sitting. • read a beginning chapter book across several sittings. • read different genres (e.g., simple biographies, simple mysteries, poetry).	• select texts that match their reading level, interests, and purposes. • keep a record of books read. • read multiple books within a series, genre, or by an author. • identify and talk about favorite series, authors, and books. • increase independent reading stamina. • identify strengths as a reader. • identify things to learn or do in order to become a better reader.
Oral Reading Fluency	• use multiple cues to problem-solve words quickly. • take words apart (onsets, rimes, endings, contractions, compound words) to decode words. • use analogies to decode words with common spelling patterns (e.g., *out*, *shout*). • quickly self-correct significant miscues. • read in longer phrases. • attend to and read basic punctuation. • read dialogue with expression. • read at an appropriate rate.	• read appropriately leveled texts with a high level of accuracy. • monitor meaning and use fix-up strategies when meaning is unclear. • search and monitor vowel patterns within words. • quickly take words apart (e.g., onsets, rimes, endings, compound words) to decode words. • identify and use familiar consonant and vowel patterns to divide two-to-three-syllable words. • use analogies to decode word segments with similar spelling patterns (e.g., *thought*, *bought*). • read with expression that conveys intended meaning. • read in longer, meaningful phrases. • adjust rate as needed.
Comprehension	• make predictions based on prior knowledge, the book title, and oral book introduction. • extract more meaning from the text; rely less on the illustrations. • monitor meaning across pages/short chapters. • recall main ideas and supporting details from previously read chapters or segments to continue constructing and monitoring meaning. • use fix-up strategies when meaning is not clear. • gain some information from text features (e.g., book/chapter titles, headings, table of contents). • understand basic information presented graphically. • identify important ideas, details, and vocabulary to include in a retelling. • retell important ideas and details sequentially or in a logical order. • identify story elements (e.g., characters, setting, problem, solution). • make text-to-self connections.	• engage with the text by accessing prior knowledge and initial information from the text to make meaningful predictions. • generate relevant questions before and during reading. • identify important ideas, details, and vocabulary to include in a summary. • compose a written summary using their own language, key ideas, and vocabulary from the text. • identify the most important event and tell why it is important. • make text-to-text and text-to-world connections. • support opinions with examples from the text or personal experience. • make inferences and discuss or record what is implied or suggested in the text. • understand the meaning of common prefixes (e.g., *re-*, *un-*) and suffixes (e.g., *-less*, *-ful*). • participate in book discussions. • understand the purpose of titles/headings, boldface words, glossary, and captions. • use titles/headings as a basis for predictions and questions. • use boldface words, glossary, and captions to clarify meaning. • skim to locate and/or recheck information. • locate and restate information within the text to respond to literal questions. • interpret information presented graphically (e.g., basic charts, graphs, maps, diagrams).

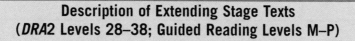

Description of Extending Stage Texts
(*DRA*2 Levels 28–38; Guided Reading Levels M–P)

Content
- wide variety of experiences, topics, and themes that go beyond Extending readers' experience
- familiar as well as specialized and/or more challenging vocabulary
- illustrations/photographs provide a moderate to low level of support
- information presented graphically in nonfiction texts (e.g., charts, graphs, timelines, maps, diagrams)
- more descriptions/details of story elements (e.g., setting, characters, and plot)

Genre/Text Structure
- wide variety of genres (e.g., realistic fiction, informational texts, mystery, fantasy, biography, historical fiction, humor, adventure, poetry)
- longer chapter books that contain short chapters
- series (e.g., *Baby-Sitters Club, Magic Tree House, Magic School Bus, Junie B. Jones*)
- informational text structures (e.g., charts, comparison/contrast, cause/effect, directions, descriptions)

Language/Word Structures
- oral, written, and literary language structures
- content-specific language
- increasing number of polysyllabic words
- more challenging vocabulary that may require readers to identify and use meaning units (base/root words and affixes) within words

Layout
- multiple lines of text per page
- full pages of print
- illustrations extend the text, depict characters and setting
- information presented graphically generally reinforces the written text
- smaller font size and spacing between words and lines of text

Extending Strategic Reading Behaviors

Scaffold (Model, Teach, and Reinforce) Extending Readers to . . .

Before Reading	• look at the title and the cover illustration and think about the text (*What is this about? What kind of book is this? What are my expectations?*). • preview texts, making predictions about what is likely to happen or identifying topics and information that may be included.
During Reading	• predict what they think will happen next; confirm and/or alter predictions. • read text with an appropriate rate, phrasing, and expression. • quickly problem-solve unknown/challenging words using multiple sources of information. • take apart longer, unknown words (e.g., syllables, endings, common letter sequences). • quickly self-correct significant miscues. • read silently. • monitor meaning across pages, segments, and/or chapters. • use fix-up strategies when meaning is not clear.
After Reading	• discuss text-to-self, text-to-text, and/or text-to-world connections made while reading. • demonstrate understanding of the characters through discussion. • interpret characters' actions, decisions, behaviors. • discuss what the author is trying to say in the story/text (message). • identify the most important thing that happened in the story. • use details from the text and personal experiences to support opinion(s). • write a "scaffolded" summary. • compare and contrast characters, stories, and texts.

Name _____   Date _____

Draw a picture of your favorite part of the story.

Tell why it is your favorite part.

_____

_____

_____

_____

Name _____   Date _____

Draw a picture in each box to show what happened in the story.

⬇
Beginning

⬇
Middle

⬇
End

Name _____ Date _____

AFTER READING

Summary

Write a summary of the story in your own words. Include the important characters, events, and details from the beginning, middle, and end of the story. Use the words and phrases below to help you organize your summary.

In the beginning, _____

_____

_____

Next, _____

_____

_____

Then, _____

_____

_____

After that, _____

_____

_____

In the end, _____

_____

_____

Name _____ Date _____

AFTER READING

SUMMARY

Write a summary of the story in your own words. Include the important characters, events, and details from the beginning, middle, and end of the story.

_____

_____

_____

_____

_____

_____

_____

_____

_____

_____

_____

_____

_____

_____

_____

_____

_____

Name _____   Date _____

Text Features

Think about the title, the pictures you have seen, and what you have read so far.

What do you know about the characters _____ and

_____ ?

_____

_____

_____

_____

Prediction

What are 2 things you think might happen in the rest of the story?

1. _____

_____

2. _____

_____

Name _____ Date _____

List 3 questions that you had while reading the first part of the book.

1. _____

_____

2. _____

_____

3. _____

_____

What are 3 things that you think might happen or that you might learn from reading the rest of the book?

1. _____

_____

2. _____

_____

3. _____

_____

Reflection

Name _____ Date _____

What is the most important event in the story?

_____

_____

_____

_____

Why do you think it is important?

_____

_____

_____

_____

Reflection

Name _____ Date _____

What do you think the author is trying to tell you in this story?

_____

_____

_____

_____

Why do you think it is important?

_____

_____

_____

_____

Metacognitive Awareness

Name _____   Date _____

Check 1 strategy that you used to help you understand the book.

- ☐   I recalled what I know about the topic.
- ☐   I asked myself questions as I read.
- ☐   I made connections.
- ☐   I decided what was important to remember.
- ☐   I thought about the reasons why things happened.
- ☐   I pictured what was happening.

Give at least 2 specific examples from this book that show how you used this comprehension strategy.

_____

_____

_____

_____

_____

Name _____ Date _____

My Book Log

Date:	Title:	
Author:		Genre:

Date:	Title:	
Author:		Genre:

Date:	Title:	
Author:		Genre:

Date:	Title:	
Author:		Genre:

Date:	Title:	
Author:		Genre:

Date:	Title:	
Author:		Genre:

Date:	Title:	
Author:		Genre:

Date:	Title:	
Author:		Genre:

Date:	Title:	
Author:		Genre:

Date:	Title:	
Author:		Genre:

Frequently Asked Questions About DRA2

For the results of *DRA2, K–3*, to be reliable and accurate, it is important for you to be familiar with the guidelines and procedures for administering the assessment. In addition to the guidelines provided in this Teacher Guide, here are answers to some of the most frequently asked questions teachers have about *DRA2* that you may find helpful.

What is the appropriate number of times to administer DRA2?

In general, the assessment is given twice a year (fall and spring) to provide teachers with information to guide instruction. There is always the option to administer the assessment more frequently. Oftentimes, the assessment is administered at mid-year to identify the needs or skills of students who are challenged readers. It is also given mid-year, in some cases, to monitor student progress and to provide more instructional guidance.

Is it okay to prompt the child and ask the child to reread with better expression?

No. When a student is reading aloud during the assessment, it is not an instructional moment. The information gained from the student's oral reading is intended to be a snapshot of the student's skills at that point in time. The teacher should use the information gleaned from the assessment to guide instruction in the weeks to come.

Do we count a word error if a child misreads the word every time it is repeated in the text?

Every error, except for the repetition of a person's name (*Raymond* for *Ramon*), is counted each time.

Does writing in the DRA2, K–3, give an accurate portrayal of comprehension?

It is true that students will not be able to write all they would tell in an oral retelling so they must determine what is most important to include in their written responses and how to organize their thoughts in a meaningful or logical order. The composing process gives students time to do so. It also enables students to reread and revise what they have written in order to clarify their understanding of what they have read and/or written. Many state assessments ask for written responses as well. The *DRA2* gives teachers insight into how well Extending readers respond in writing.

How can DRA2 help me meet the needs of students in special education?

DRA2 can help to address students' IEP goals and objectives. For example, the DRA Continuum can be immediately turned into measurable goals and objectives.

Are there any parts of DRA2 that can be omitted and still maintain the integrity of the test?

No. The assessment was field-tested and revised based on the field-test feedback. One of the strengths of *DRA2* is that a student reads the entire text as opposed to an excerpt. This helps the student construct meaning or comprehend across extended text (beginning, middle, and end). The student is able to respond with more depth because more information and context is provided. This task resembles real-life reading.

How much should fluency be weighed in the earliest levels?

When students are just beginning to decode, they are less fluent because they are learning how to analyze and take words apart while constructing meaning. As students become more proficient in problem-solving unknown words, they become more fluent. In *DRA2* it is recommended that students read at least 30 words per minute beginning with Level 14. Students do read at different rates. Fluency becomes a concern when a student reads so slowly that it is difficult to gain enough momentum to comprehend. Allington, as well as Fountas and Pinnell, cite sources that suggest that by the end of first grade students should be reading approximately 60 words per minute. Fluency also impacts students' perceptions of themselves as readers and the amount they are able to read at any given time.

Recommended References

*DRA*2 was created to assess and document primary students' development as readers over time. Knowing how to create rich literate environments and learning experiences that honor the way children learn is also essential in establishing an effective early literacy learning program.

The following professional books are recommended as a means to guide and extend your understanding of effective ways to teach reading/writing in primary grades (K–3).

Allington, Richard L. *What Really Matters for Struggling Readers: Designing Research-Based Programs* (Second Edition). New York, NY: Allyn & Bacon, 2005.

Bamford, Rosemary A., and Janice V. Kristo. *Checking Out Nonfiction K–8: Good Choices for Best Learning.* Norwood, MA: Christopher-Gordon Publishers, 2000.

Bamford, Rosemary A., and Janice V. Kristo. *Making Facts Come Alive: Choosing Quality Nonfiction Literature K–8*. Norwood, MA: Christopher-Gordon Publishers, 1998.

Bear, Donald R., Marcie Invernizzi, Shane Templeton, and Francine Johnston. *Words Their Way: Word Study for Phonics, Vocabulary, and Spelling Instruction*. Upper Saddle River, NJ: Pearson, 2004.

Benson, Vicki, and Carrice Cummins. *The Power of Retelling: Developmental Steps for Building Comprehension*. Bothell, WA: Wright Group/McGraw-Hill, 2000.

Brand, Max. *Word Savvy: Integrated Vocabulary, Spelling, & Word Study, Grades 3–6*. Portland, ME: Stenhouse Publishers, 2004.

Calkins, Lucy McCormick. *The Art of Teaching Reading*. New York, NY: Allyn & Bacon, 2000.

Clay, Marie M. *An Observation Survey of Early Literacy Achievement* (Second Edition). Portsmouth, NH: Heinemann, 2002.

Cunningham, Patricia M. *Phonics They Use: Words for Reading and Writing* (Fourth Edition). New York, NY: Allyn & Bacon, 2004.

Daniels, Harvey, and Nancy Steineke. *Mini-Lessons for Literature Circles*. Portsmouth, NH: Heinemann, 2004.

Duke, Nell K., and V. Susan Bennett-Amistead. *Reading & Writing Informational Text in the Primary Grades: Research-Based Practices*. New York, NY: Scholastic Teaching Resources, 2003.

Fisher, Bobbi, and Emily Fisher Medvic. *For Reading Out Loud: Planning and Practice*. Portsmouth, NH: Heinemann, 2003.

Fountas, Irene C., and Gay Su Pinnell. *Matching Books to Readers: Using Leveled Books in Guided Reading, K–3*. Portsmouth, NH: Heinemann, 1999.

Fountas, Irene C., and Gay Su Pinnell. *Guided Reading: Good First Teaching for All Children*. Portsmouth, NH: Heinemann, 1996.

Harvey, Stephanie, and Anne Goudvis. *Strategies That Work: Teaching Comprehension to Enhance Understanding*. York, ME: Stenhouse Publishers, 2000.

Hebert, Dr. Connie R. *Catch a Falling Reader: A Daily Guide for Teachers & Parents*. Bloomington, IN: AuthorHouse, 2005.

Herrell, Adrienne, and Michael Jordan. *Fifty Strategies for Teaching English Language Learners* (Second Edition). Upper Saddle River, NJ: Prentice Hall, 2003.

Hoyt, Linda. *Make It Real: Strategies for Success with Informational Texts*. Portsmouth, NH: Heinemann, 2002.

Hoyt, Linda. *Revisit, Reflect, Retell: Strategies for Improving Reading Comprehension*. Portsmouth, NH: Heinemann, 1998.

Hoyt, Linda, and Margaret Mooney and Brenda Parkes, eds. *Exploring Informational Texts: From Theory to Practice*. Portsmouth, NH: Heinemann, 2003.

Keene, Ellin Oliver, and Susan Zimmermann. *Mosaic of Thought: Teaching Comprehension in a Reader's Workshop*. Portsmouth, NH: Heinemann, 1997.

Lyons, Carol A. *Teaching Struggling Readers: How to Use Brain-based Research to Maximize Learning*. Portsmouth, NH: Heinemann, 2003.

McCarrier, Andrea, Gay Su Pinnell, and Irene C. Fountas. *Interactive Writing: How Language & Literacy Come Together, K–2*. Portsmouth, NH: Heinemann, 1999.

McLaughlin, Maureen, and Glenn DeVoogd. *Critical Literacy: Enhancing Students' Comprehension of Text*. New York, NY: Scholastic Inc., 2004.

Miller, Debbie. *Reading with Meaning: Teaching Comprehension in the Primary Grades*. Portland, ME: Stenhouse Publishers, 2002.

Moline, Steve. *I See What You Mean: Children at Work with Visual Information*. York, ME: Stenhouse Publishers, 1995.

Morrow, Lesley Mandel. *The Literacy Center: Contexts for Reading and Writing*, (Second Edition). Portland, ME: Stenhouse Publishers, 2002.

Parkes, Brenda. *Read It Again!: Revisiting Shared Reading*. Portland, ME: Stenhouse, 2000.

Pinnell, Gay Su, and Patricia L. Scharer. *Teaching for Comprehension in Reading Grades K–2: Strategies for Helping Children Read With Ease, Confidence, and Understanding*. New York, NY: Scholastic Inc., 2003.

Rasinski, Timothy, and Nancy Padak. *From Phonics to Fluency: Effective Teaching of Decoding and Reading Fluency in the Elementary School*. New York, NY: Allyn & Bacon, 2000.

Routman, Regie. *Reading Essentials: The Specifics You Need to Teach Reading Well*. Portsmouth, NH: Heinemann, 2002.

Routman, Regie. *Conversations: Strategies for Teaching, Learning, and Evaluating*. Portsmouth, NH: Heinemann, 1999.

Sibberson, Franki, and Karen Szymusiak. *Still Learning to Read: Teaching Students in Grades 3–6*. Portland, ME: Stenhouse Publishers, 2003.

Stead, Tony. *Is That a Fact?: Teaching Nonfiction Writing K–3*, Portland, ME: Stenhouse Publishers, 2001.

Strickland, Dorothy S., Kathy Ganske, and Joanne K. Monroe. *Supporting Struggling Readers and Writers: Strategies for Classroom Intervention 3–6*. Portland, ME: Stenhouse, 2001.

Szymusiak, Karen, and Franki Sibberson. *Beyond Leveled Books: Supporting Transitional Readers in Grades 2–5*. Portland, ME: Stenhouse Publishers, 2001.

Taberski, Sharon. *On Solid Ground: Strategies for Teaching Reading K–3*. Portsmouth, NH: Heinemann, 2000.

Wollman-Bonilla, Julie. *Family Message Journals: Teaching Writing through Family Involvement*. Urbana, IL: National Council of Teachers of English, 2000.

Recommended References

Record of Oral Reading Guidelines

Reading Behavior	How to Record Observed Behavior	Examples	Number of Errors
Accurate Reading	No notation	An octopus has no backbone	No errors
Substitution	Record substitution	*beginning* tears begin to well up	*Each substitution is counted as one error.
Repetition	Insert *R* and an arrow to indicate word(s) repeated or underline word(s) repeated	Always looking for a Mike <u>was</u> <u>thoroughly</u>	Repetitions are **not counted as errors** but impact fluency.
Self-Correction	Insert *sc* after substitution	*discovered/sc* They described the weather	Self-corrections are not counted as errors.
Omission	Circle omitted word(s)	One day, as she and ⟨her⟩ mother …	Each omission is counted as one error.
Insertion	Use a caret to record added word(s)	*the* covered in ^ snow and ice.	Each inserted word is counted as one error.
Reversals	Use the reversal symbol when words are reversed	She quickly ⌣agreed to	A reversal is counted as one error.
Sounding Out	Record letter sounds and use slash marks to show how words were segmented	Princess was cap|tiv|ated… …uses a fun|nel for…	**Words sounded out incorrectly are counted as one error.
Word Told by Teacher	Insert a *T* above word(s) told	T many disguises and and tricks	Each word told by the teacher is counted as one error.
Long Pauses	Insert a *W* above the places, or use slash marks, where student pauses	W They got a bucket They saw/some/cashews	Pauses are **not counted as errors** but impact fluency.

* **Repeated Substitutions:** If the child makes an error (e.g., *run* for *ran*) and then substitutes this word repeatedly, it counts as an error every time. The substitution of a proper name (e.g., *Mary* for *Molly*) is counted as an error only the first time.
* Substitutions involving contractions count as one error.   Examples: I will   I'll
                                                                                      I'll   *I will*

** **Words mispronounced due to a speech problem or dialect** may be coded but are not counted as errors.
         Examples: git   pitcher   are
                          get   *picture*   *our*

Note: Miscues of numerals and abbreviations are not to be counted in the total number of miscues, but they can be noted for future instruction.

Words Per Minute Chart

NOTE: Ranges for Levels 2 through 12 are Emerging, Developing, Independent, and Advanced

Texts	Level	Genre	pp.	Words Full TXT	Words ROR	WPM INTERVN	WPM INSTR	WPM IND	WPM ADV	% INTERVN	% INSTR	% IND	% ADV
Can You Sing?	A	F	16	42	10					70 or less	80	90–100	
Things That Go	1	F	12	20	16					81 or less	88	94–100	
What Is Red?	1	F	12	20	16					81 or less	88	94–100	
Bath Time	2	F	16	40	34					88 or less	91	94–100	
I Can See	2	F	16	42	36					89 or less	92	94–100	
The "I Like" Game	3	F	16	54	46					89 or less	91	93–100	
Look at Me	3	F	16	58	49					90 or less	92	94–100	
Get Your Umbrella	4	F	8	53	53					91 or less	92	94–96	98–100
Where Is My Hat?	4	F	8	54	54					91 or less	93	94–96	98–100
Time to Play	6	F	8	72	72					92 or less	93	94–97	99–100
Why Are We Stopping?	6	F	8	73	73					92 or less	93	95–97	99–100
Duke	8	F	8	87	87					92 or less	93	94–97	98–100
The Lost Book	8	F	8	90	90					92 or less	93	94–97	98–100
Grandma's Surprise	10	F	8	127	127					92 or less	93	94–97	98–100
Shoe Boxes	10	F	8	130	130					92 or less	93	94–97	98–100
Allie's Wish	12	F	8	134	134					92 or less	93	94–97	98–100
Robert's New Friend	12	F	8	137	137					92 or less	93	94–97	98–100
A New School	14	F	8	207	207	29 or less	30–39	40–70	71 or more	93 or less	94	95–98	99–100
The Wagon	14	F	8	202	202	29 or less	30–39	40–70	71 or more	93 or less	94	95–98	99–100
Animal Homes	16	NF	16	174	174	29 or less	30–39	40–70	71 or more	93 or less	94	95–98	99–100
Baby Birds	16	NF	16	177	177	29 or less	30–39	40–70	71 or more	93 or less	94	95–98	99–100
Chip to the Rescue	16	F	8	253	253	34 or less	35–44	45–75	76 or more	93 or less	94	95–98	99–100
Monkey's Stepping Stones	16	F	8	258	258	34 or less	35–44	45–75	76 or more	93 or less	94	95–98	99–100
Game Day	18	F	8	278	141	44 or less	45–54	55–85	86 or more	93 or less	94	95–98	99–100
A Giant in the Forest	18	F	8	278	134	44 or less	45–54	55–85	86 or more	93 or less	94	95–98	99–100
Green Freddie	20	F	8	426	153	54 or less	55–64	65–95	96 or more	93 or less	94	95–98	99–100
Turtle's Big Race	20	F	8	401	147	54 or less	55–64	65–95	96 or more	93 or less	94	95–98	99–100
Thin as a Stick	24	F	8	458	170	59 or less	60–69	70–100	101 or more	93 or less	94	95–98	99–100
The Wonderful Day	24	F	8	466	172	59 or less	60–69	70–100	101 or more	93 or less	94	95–98	99–100
Animals Can Help	28	NF	16	425	143	64 or less	65–74	75–105	106 or more	93 or less	94	95–98	99–100
From Peanuts to Peanut Butter	28	NF	16	423	168	64 or less	65–74	75–105	106 or more	93 or less	94	95–98	99–100
Missing Sneakers	28	F	8	688	196	64 or less	65–74	75–105	106 or more	93 or less	94	95–98	99–100
You Don't Look Beautiful to Me	28	F	8	689	176	64 or less	65–74	75–105	106 or more	93 or less	94	95–98	99–100
Busy Helpers	30	F	12	963	216	69 or less	65–79	80–110	111 or more	94 or less	95	96–98	99–100
Tiger's Whirlwind Day	30	F	12	971	228	69 or less	65–79	80–110	111 or more	94 or less	95	96–98	99–100
The Mystery at the Mays' House	34	F	12	1080	216	64 or less	65–79	80–115	116 or more	94 or less	95	96–98	99–100
Summer Discovery	34	F	12	1036	214	64 or less	65–79	80–115	116 or more	94 or less	95	96–98	99–100
Mae Jemison	38	NF	16	819	210	69 or less	70–89	90–125	126 or more	94 or less	95	96–98	99–100
Slammin' Sammy	38	NF	16	831	221	69 or less	70–89	90–125	126 or more	94 or less	95	96–98	99–100
A Trip Through Time	38	F	12	1064	223	69 or less	70–89	90–125	126 or more	94 or less	95	96–98	99–100
Trouble at the Beaver Pond	38	F	12	1089	227	69 or less	70–89	90–125	126 or more	94 or less	95	96–98	99–100
All the Way Under	40	F	12	1359	255	74 or less	75–104	105–140	141 or more	95 or less	96	97–98	99–100
The Amazing Octopus	40	NF	12	941	189	69 or less	70–99	100–135	136 or more	95 or less	96	97–98	99–100
A Journey to Freedom	40	F	12	1325	253	74 or less	75–104	105–140	141 or more	95 or less	96	97–98	99–100
A Pack of Wolves	40	NF	12	992	205	69 or less	70–99	100–135	136 or more	95 or less	96	97–98	99–100

Thank you for purchasing the
Developmental Reading Assessment®

Return this card today to join the DRA2 Community of educators.

Your Name:_____

School Name:_____

School Address: _____

City: _____State: _____Zip: _____County: _____

School Phone Number: (_____)_____Country: _____

Preferred Email Address:_____

1. I am a:
- ☐ Classroom Teacher
- ☐ Federal Funds Coordinator
- ☐ Assessment Coordinator
- ☐ Curriculum Supervisor
- ☐ ESL/ELL Teacher
- ☐ Homeschooler
- ☐ Special Education Teacher
- ☐ Principal/Administrator
- ☐ Other_____

2. The DRA programs I am using are (Check all that apply):
- ☐ DRA2 K-3
- ☐ DRA K-3 Original
- ☐ DRA Word Analysis
- ☐ DRA K-3 Alternative Text
- ☐ DRA2 4-8
- ☐ DRA 4-8
- ☐ DRA 4-8 Bridge Pack
- ☐ EDL K-3
- ☐ DRA Online Management System
- ☐ DRA Leveled Library
- ☐ DWA

3. I teach (Check all that apply):
- ☐ Kindergarten
- ☐ Grade 1
- ☐ Grade 2
- ☐ Grade 3
- ☐ Grade 4
- ☐ Grade 5
- ☐ Grade 6
- ☐ Grade 7
- ☐ Grade 8
- ☐ Special Education
- ☐ Other_____

4. I will use DRA to (Check all that apply):
- ☐ Get students' reading levels
- ☐ Monitor students' progress
- ☐ Other_____
- ☐ Determine students' instructional needs and create flexible groups
- ☐ Diagnose students' reading problems

5. In my school, DRA is used:
- ☐ Only in my classroom
- ☐ As part of a district initiative
- ☐ In collaboration with other teachers
- ☐ As part of a state initiative
- ☐ As part of a school initiative

6. I heard about DRA through:
- ☐ Sales Rep
- ☐ Catalog/Brochure
- ☐ Another Teacher
- ☐ Educational Conference
- ☐ My Administrator
- ☐ Other_____
- ☐ Literature
- ☐ Website

7. Did you purchase DRA though a Grant? ☐ Yes ☐ No
Please list the Grant(s): _____

8. I would like more information about the following programs:
- ☐ DRA2 K-3
- ☐ DRA Word Analysis
- ☐ DRA2 Online Management System
- ☐ Little Celebrations
- ☐ Book Treks
- ☐ DRA2 4-8
- ☐ EDL K-3
- ☐ Celebrations Grade Level Libraries
- ☐ Reading With Strategies
- ☐ DRA Leveled Libraries
- ☐ DWA
- ☐ Chatterbox
- ☐ iOpeners

9. I am interested in (Check all that apply):
- ☐ Receiving the *DRA InfoLink*, the DRA newsletter
- ☐ Participating in studies for future DRA products

To complete mailer, fold and seal with adhesive tape. Do not staple. *Thank you.*

Return This Card Now and Become a Member of the DRA2 Community.

Member Benefits include:

✔ **Subscription to the *DRA InfoLink***

This newsletter provides educators with the latest DRA information, practical instructional strategies to use after assessments, and DRA Online tips.

✔ **Previews of Future DRA Products**

As a DRA member, you'll be invited to preview and/or field test upcoming DRA products.

✔ **Special Offers**

Receive notification of special savings on DRA and other Pearson Learning Group products.

Modern Curriculum Press
Globe Fearon
Celebration Press
Dominie Press
Dale Seymour Publications
Pearson Early Learning

Visit Our Website to Register Online: www.DRAHome.com